Praise for Reshaping the Paradigm... ...ing and Learning

"Dr. Wimberley shares thoughtful insights and knowledge about education for this unprecedented time in our society where our children will grow up as digital natives. All educators who want more for their students need to read this book."
—**Dean Tagawa**, executive director of early childhood education, Los Angeles Unified School District, Los Angeles, California

"*Reshaping the Paradigms of Teaching and Learning* is a must-read for every aspiring or current educational leader. The context of education demands change. Dr. Wimberley challenges us as educational leaders to break the constraints of our institutionalized teaching system by embracing the twenty-first-century ideals of teaching and learning."
—**Ryan S. Saxe**, executive director of secondary schools, School District of Manatee County, Florida

"Dr. Alan Wimberley enthusiastically highlights the future steps to student learning in the United States. *Reshaping the Paradigms of Teaching and Learning* has opened my mind to real twenty-first-century learning and the unlimited opportunities for changing our traditional instructional delivery system. I encourage educational leaders and all stakeholders to read this thoughtful, inspiring look at educational reform."
—**Rick Neal**, superintendent, Pea Ridge School District, Pea Ridge, Arkansas

"In *Reshaping the Paradigms of Teaching and Learning*, Dr. Wimberley takes readers on a thoughtful journey providing a glimpse of current deficiencies within the education system, and pronounces imperative changes. Principally, he shifts priorities, and masterfully creates an architectural blueprint for education sure to create an effective educational paradigm shift on a national scale for the future. I would highly recommend this powerful visionary reading as it evoked emotions from me as an educational leader to fulfill my part in navigating positive change."
—**Shawntrice Z. Thomas**, EdD, assistant professor of Education

"The most powerful model for building a better future for our youth, and essentially our country, is to reshape the public educational process, particularly for poor students. Dr. Wimberley challenges our traditional approach, and beliefs, of an ailing system in this read. Educators everywhere should welcome such refreshing insight and take action going forward to build better opportunities for our students."
—**Jon Collins**, superintendent, West Memphis School District, West Memphis, Arkansas

RESHAPING THE PARADIGMS OF TEACHING AND LEARNING

Thank you for changing the lives of kids

Alan Wimberley

4-19

RESHAPING THE PARADIGMS OF TEACHING AND LEARNING

What Happens Today Is Education's Future

Alan Wimberley

ROWMAN & LITTLEFIELD
Lanham • Boulder • New York • London

Published by Rowman & Littlefield
A wholly owned subsidiary of The Rowman & Littlefield Publishing Group, Inc.
4501 Forbes Boulevard, Suite 200, Lanham, Maryland 20706
www.rowman.com

Unit A, Whitacre Mews, 26-34 Stannary Street, London SE11 4AB

British Library Cataloguing in Publication Information Available

Library of Congress Cataloging-in-Publication Data

Names: Wimberley, Alan, 1959- author.
Title: Reshaping the paradigms of teaching and learning : what happens today is education's future / Alan Wimberley.
Description: Lanham : Rowman & Littlefield, [2016] | Includes bibliographical references.
Identifiers: LCCN 2016015798 (print) | LCCN 2016028521 (ebook) | ISBN 9781475826562 (cloth : alk. paper) | ISBN 9781475826579 (pbk. : alk. paper) | ISBN 9781475826586 (Electronic)
Subjects: LCSH: Educational change--United States.
Classification: LCC LA217.2 .W555 2016 (print) | LCC LA217.2 (ebook) | DDC 370.73--dc23
LC record available at https://lccn.loc.gov/2016015798

∞ ™ The paper used in this publication meets the minimum requirements of American National Standard for Information Sciences—Permanence of Paper for Printed Library Materials, ANSI/NISO Z39.48-1992.

Printed in the United States of America

To Bonnie Belle,
the best teacher I've known and my sweet wife,
and our wonderful tribe of children and grandchildren.
Each of you defines adventurous learning for me.

CONTENTS

ACKNOWLEDGMENTS

I've had the opportunity to work with, walk with, and learn from incredible people. No one knows everything and it's only through the collective investment and sacrifice of these individuals that I know anything at all.

My greatest relationships have been formed when there was a bond of mutual learning among those I count as my closest friends in this work. No book on these issues would be possible without the bond and friendship I have with Charles Cook. Chuck and I have worked together for a number of years, and just sharing the same passion and hope for kids, parents, and teachers keeps me engaged and focused. He is more than a friend; he is the anchor for much of my work.

I count the men and women at Responsive Education Solutions to be the greatest examples of those who give themselves for kids every day. They certainly "draw the maps" for education in my life and just being around them makes me better.

To Robert Davison, for making sure it all operates the way it should.

Dr. Steve Bourgeois must be acknowledged for the tremendous help and guidance he provided for me throughout the writing of this book.

I owe so much to so many.

To my publisher, Dr. Tom Koerner, you, more than most, have encouraged me with your support, your wisdom, and your belief in this work.

To the many at Rowman and Littlefield, including Carlie Wall, who answered every question and guided every step, I am genuinely grateful.

To Dr. Bob Maranto, my lunch partner, my confidante and my trusted counsel, you continue to be a source of good change for kids and schools.

To Dr. John Brooks, my mentor and friend, you pushed me when it was important.

To Dr. Shawntrice Thomas, who taught me that we are better teachers when we choose to never stop learning.

To brave superintendents like Rick Neal and Jon Collins for knowing there's more we can do for kids and for taking the risks to do it.

To those policymakers and politicians, district administrators and teachers, charter educators, private school teachers, and homeschool parents, may each of you know that the sacrifice you make each day is recognized and honorable.

Lastly, to my hometown teachers, brothers and friends, college instructors, and university professors . . . thank you for being patient.

PREFACE

You Will Want to Read This First

Outside our front door is a world full of children created for learning. They depend on us and trust us to do what's best for them. They are why we do what we do. Every generation takes on the responsibility to pass on knowledge (and hopefully wisdom) to the next generation. It's never meant to be a job. It should be approached as a sacred and exciting way to spend your life: handing off the important things to those who will hand them off to others after we're gone.

We stand at an interesting place right now in education. If you spend your days in a classroom, be grateful. *You are the best part of our educational hope*. There is nothing more encouraging than actually walking among the young and performing the miracle of teaching.

However, if you are one of those working outside that classroom, whether it be standing on the floor of the Capitol, sitting around the tables at the state office, or walking the hallways at central administration, you need to know (or be reminded) that so much of what we do in those arenas of education is more about adults than children. All in the name of "we love the kids," "we want to do what's best for children," we pontificate, we politic, and we parlay our ideas, our beliefs, and our prejudices, all in the name of "doing what's best for kids." You, me, all of us.

Now if you don't think that's true, just pay close attention. A lot of what we do outside that classroom has more to do with adults than children. Give it your litmus test. Is this about kids or adults? Ask yourself that question every time. We spend a lot of time trying to satisfy our idea of what is and isn't, what should and shouldn't, and what will and won't.

We spend millions of dollars every year putting intelligent adults in rooms to strategize and construct tests that, rather than assessing what kids do and don't know, will intricately "trick" kids. We call it higher order critical thinking and rigor. We spend hours and days and weeks training kids how to pass these tests. We create high-level security procedures to keep adults from cheating the system.

We construct accountability rules and data slicing that no one can even understand. We measure schools, not kids. We fight on every issue that comes along and take a lot of time arguing about things that have nothing to do with children. An adult runs for the school board so that they can fire an adult at the school and make other adults in the community happy. We have created a double-edged industrial sword of "education" and "education reform." It puts bread on our tables. The education industry is massive, powerful, and filled with adults.

Yet every day, thousands of doors close and a teacher stands alone in a room full of kids. And no matter how much self-importance we grant ourselves, at the end of the day, that room is all that matters. It's simple: what goes on in that classroom that day will make the difference in that child that day. Education is really about one thing: passing knowledge to a child; working with a child; and giving our best to a child.

What we do in education is important. And bread on the table for adults working with students is important. But we really can get lost in all this. And we can forget that we are secondary to that classroom. We can forget that our efforts and our work are not the most important thing. In our positions of power and authority, we can forget that kid. But that kid matters.

We have an interesting dynamic in education now. We work in an industry where we can admit failure, but not in our backyard. We work in an industry where we can agree that it needs change, but not on our campus. We work in an industry that piles on regulations and rules for adults and, sometimes, those rules and regulations actually make their way down through the tunnels of the system and affect the kids, but more often than not, they don't make too much difference. Because every morning that door closes and it's that teacher with those children. What happens that day makes the difference that day.

THE PURPOSE

So why another book to just say what's already being said? There's already more than enough books articulating what's wrong, why it's wrong, and how wrong it is. Why read this one? And, even more interesting, why even write it? No doubt there will be no revolutionary new idea shared here. There's no epiphany, or as some call it, their "aha moment" within these pages. So why even write it?

For two reasons: 1) we have a generation of educators being trained who have the capacity to use new resources and ideas, but we continue to train this generation in much the same systems we've always trained and 2) we are at a crucial stage where a generation of children have known nothing but a digital world since childbirth. The immediate need to address the incapacity of traditional teaching systems as related to these two generational layers demands we reshape our paradigm now.

It's a tremendous privilege to teach educators. Those who have taught children throughout their years of work serve us well when they invest themselves in later years to teaching those who will teach future generations. While knowing that ongoing professional development is needed for current practice and skills, an experienced generation of educators taking on the role of craftsmen teaching future educators as apprentices is invaluable. Teaching those who will teach children is important.

THE VIEW FROM THE TEACHER'S DESK

The bureaucracy of being in a teaching system can often kill the passion and make teachers feel defeated. And when talking about genuine change in education, there's the "shaking head of yes" of practitioners when research is presented and the "wagging finger of no" when real change is actually considered as a reality. There are volumes of findings, reports, and data. But teachers experience, see, and listen to children and adolescents when they have actually learned something they didn't know before.

The tasking demands of a teaching system will make you weary and worn. But the excitement of learning cannot be replaced or replicated anywhere other than that classroom, where they sit and wait to see what we're going to do.

This is written from the perspective of someone who teaches current trends and issues to educators. Nothing is more current than the issues presented in this book. It's a strange time to be an educator. The last century saw the institutionalization of a created system of education that consumed and convinced us that this was the way all students were supposed to learn.

This system became so all-consuming that anything presented now in this new century is defined and valued according to the former century's definitions and ideas. We place everything up against that measuring stick and proclaim its significance (or lack thereof) on how it affects, or meets the standards of, our entrenched system of teaching that somehow became our adopted practice.

We already have wonderful research, books, and other literature targeting the need for current implementation and opportunity in education. The authors have already shown us the way. The roadmaps have already been drawn. The problem is that we just aren't making aggressive headway to revolutionize our educational system. We are still training our teachers in the former methodologies. So we train them and place them in the system and, eventually, they find themselves shaking the head and wagging the finger.

Honestly, when you add a headshake of yes to a wagging finger of no, it ends up where it always ends up—a shoulder shrug. "What can we do? This is the reality of the real world." Shrug the shoulder, shrug it off, and keep spinning the wheels of safe systems that will leave kids behind; but at least the majority will be saved.

We have so many great works to introduce and expose education students to the challenges faced in current trends and issues. However, because we have most likely been presented with these issues during our learning journey, we know that these issues exist, but we have been trained in such a way that we can give a cursory agreement to the need while not really intending to upend the established way we do things once we get out there.

We need a formula to get to transformation. And the first step for that formula is to intentionally introduce and expose our generation of educators to the idea that we should move to a total transformation of our paradigms about education. This book is an attempt to stretch across the issues we've been discussing for years and introduce the challenge to go beyond reforming education and do what we have to do in this new paradigm.

THE VIEW FROM THE FAVORITE CHAIR

So many people who have lived through the transition from a nondigital to a digital world are astonished and awed by technology. Our grandchildren are growing up in a world that takes it for granted. Their vocabulary, their toys, and their world are not changing. It's changed already. Any pre-warnings about this changing world are late. It's already here and it's shaping a world that isn't just an improved version of the previous world. It's an exponentially different world.

Examples of trying to navigate this world can be found in the "Doc's Story" section at the beginning of the chapters in this volume, trying to make the leap to this new world that seems to come so easily to those children. The very structure of that world is undergirded with an understanding that change is no longer a part of life—change is life.

That being the case, we know that the typical years of schooling our grandchildren will have, though still characterized by the same struggles we all faced, are going to look different and act differently. Every facet of life will be different than it was when we were young and in high school.

The greatest fear is that they will be forced into an educational system that will protect and guard a traditional model that still acts much like it's always acted. Many will argue that it already *looks* different. That may be true, but a close look at the pieces will show that it continues to *act* the same.

That system was good when it was needed. However, those days are gone. Yet we find that, through intimidation and illogical argument, the basic structural elements of that system still reign over our educational environments.

So if anything we can do or say moves us even closer to the day when real change occurs and our system is transformed into a true personalized opportunity for learners, we should do it and say it. We should desperately want these generations to learn. We should want them to love learning. We should want them to be engaged with all of life. And in a teaching system, they don't have to love learning or be engaged. *In a teaching system, they just have to pass.*

These generations, preschoolers now, will one day be sitting in that room, the door will close, and it will be that teacher with that child. We have to teach them to be young men and women of character rather than just being fed "self-esteem mantras." They need to be excited with the process of learning. They should know that learning is an adventure that becomes a lifestyle and never disengage from that adventure.

Schooling is a system. And we never want them to be in a system that demands they "learn" the teacher to survive or thrive. We never want them to be forced into the same system that worked for us, but cannot meet the demands of a new century filled with opportunity.

We don't want them to just do PowerPoints and take cool notes that they can email to their home computers while their school proclaims itself as an innovative campus. We shouldn't want them to be in the middle of so much creativity outside of school yet strangled by a systemic management system every time they enter the door of the classroom.

So just consider this an honest effort by an old teacher wanting to help his students and an old granddad wanting to leave a better world for his children's children. Now beyond that, if anyone else gets anything else out of this, all the better.

STANDING AT THE EDGE

Hopefully, you will see that every principle delineated in this book applies across the board and needs implementation now. This isn't a "before it's too late" statement. When it comes to the serious and aggressive creation of a transformed education system in this country, we have to know that *it will happen*. The current system cannot sustain itself much longer. It would be nice to think that the day will come when it's not the outliers and disrupters alone bucking the system.

It would certainly be preferable that traditional education and educators will launch a credible effort to stop shaking the head in agreement while fighting authentic and transformative change: to think differently in a collegial, positive way.

Sadly, though, that may not be the case. It will be difficult at best for entrenched educational professionals to let go of what they've been taught and trained. They trusted that what they had been told was the way it should be done. And it will go against everything they believe to deviate from that training. The impersonal "system" of schooling refuses to let go, give space, or consider anything that will replace it as the adopted environment for educating our young.

There will be some concessions; some we already have out there. There will be small, isolated pockets of innovation. By and large, though, we will continue to see what we see now: cool looking, cool sounding technology purchases and plans that are deployed only to support, and work within, the traditional system. It doesn't work. Computers are not the answer; they're only the tools of transformation. But tools of transformation are only sources of frustration if the wrong decisions for their use are made.

The change has come; we just haven't fully accepted it yet. The transformation hasn't happened because we only use the things that can make it happen to modify a system that will eventually have to transform. So will it be a positive, collegial changeover? Most likely not. The fear is that, rather than softly sliding into the transformation, educators who today have the option of welcoming the coming model of schooling will one day soon see that choice disappear.

The tide will shift and there will come *forced transformation*. If that's the case, so be it. It may come when the current generation of educators, those of us who control it now, moves on and the digital generations move from being our students to being our teachers. They will welcome it because it's all they've known. They won't see it as disruption or alternative. So it's coming but most are not sure exactly how it will play out.

This is an attempt to create a balanced approach for educators to know where we are and know that the transformation must happen systemically. Not just classrooms projects and district experiments. The change has happened but it's still considered "out of the box" and "off the wall," risky and different. That will change soon. But the change has to occur systemically: across the board, wholesale, and district-wide. Hopefully, some of the things here can help us understand that it's possible.

Meanwhile, what will happen to our generations of experienced educators who honestly want to do what's best for kids? Will we hang on to the way we were taught and trained? Will we continue using, however awkwardly, the technology that we can slowly comprehend and manipulate but we certainly won't sell out to it? Will we give some space in our classrooms for the new, but not turn over those classrooms to an entirely new way of doing what we do?

The fact is, there are many in education who shouldn't be there. In the old industrial teaching system, so many got in who didn't belong. Teachers are a funny lot. They know there are those counted among us who don't belong, who are bad for kids, and who shouldn't be in the classroom. Yet one mention of that out loud and everybody gets offended. Every teacher bristles and rises up to challenge the outrageous and offensive individual who would dare say that there are bad teachers who should get out right now.

It's as if we would rather let them stay in the classroom than admit that there might be blemishes on our system of certifying and approving someone who doesn't belong. But we do have them. And certification from an entity that has never met the person only gives endorsement and entitlement, not skill or capacity.

Some belong and some don't. And a teaching system makes it easy to do the work and tasks even if you don't like kids, don't care about engagement with learners, and don't know how to motivate students. But just as there are those who don't belong, the overwhelming majority do. *Our profession is largely filled with passionate people who have huge dreams for kids. And they show up every day wanting to change lives. And that's a sacred life to live.*

So what will happen to us in this new education system? If we hang on to the old idea that our job is to possess the content and make all the decisions about when and how much of that content is to be doled out each day, trying to keep it organized, we will be replaced. Our roles will change, but our significance will not, unless we force the issue by hanging on to the idea that we make the decisions on these parts of the job. Because no matter how important we may think this aspect of the job is, or has been, in the process, technology can, does, and will do a better job of it than we can, are, and will in the future.

So what is our role? Hopefully, we can see that in this book. It's an honest attempt to lay out the plan for two things. The first is to show a systemic way to implement the already-present change that's so often being marginalized and isolated. The second is just as important: to encourage teachers to understand the changes and challenges and embrace the fact that these are good changes that offer the best opportunity you've ever had to use all this and make the great things you do available to more kids.

You've always been able to influence, affect, and change lives. No one questions that. However, that has always been limited to a small circle and a short list of those you teach. Now if you use what's available, you're going to have the ability to reach more and change more lives. It doesn't matter whether you accept that or believe that. It's just true.

Knowing the changes that have already happened and that the day is coming when we will not have the ability to choose or decide whether to implement those changes, why not accept the challenge? Why not be the generation of educators that actually does it? Why not, instead of waiting for your district or your principal to plan it and organize it to death, start doing it? Why not, instead of waiting until enough time passes that we get to retire before the forced change happens, start it? There is no way to comprehend how much good we'll do for more kids.

Again, no one questions that you want to help kids. There's no question that you are helping kids. But what if you can help more? It will take you back to the years when you had to learn new things and be open to doing things differently. But the benefits for a greater number of learners are worth it. The kids will get it. And when the change becomes the norm, *the widespread national system*, we will see more students having opportunity. Our greatest hope is that we will help make sure no teacher is left behind.

This book provides a flow that attempts to lay out the issue in an organized fashion. Hopefully, it can give you a sense of where we are, where we need to go, and what immediate changes we should be considering to get there. There are exciting days ahead of us and, once established, our system of being able to give each kid authentic opportunity leveraging the best of all we have will be a reality. Only then can we begin to fully address the challenges and create real change.

This is an attempt to help you understand that we would not want to leave any teacher behind, unless you shouldn't stay in the game. There will be some who just won't want to make it work for kids. There will be some who can't or won't accept that everything they've believed was the foundation of their success for years isn't true and reliable. But know this: it was true then and remains true. If the foundation was built on the fact that your success is your passion for doing whatever it takes for kids, that doesn't change or go away. It remains firm in the pages of this book. If the foundation was built on the fact that your success is your ability to engage and build relationships with learners that can change their lives, that doesn't change. It's in here.

But make no mistake. If your foundation as a teacher has been built on a set of skills as a planner, presenter, and performer, that will be where the wheels will come off. Your ability to deliver content and information will have to take a backseat to our need to provide a personalized opportunity for every learner. And if you have the need to defend a traditional system that teaches, whether learning happens or not, you will have difficulty here. You may be left behind. It's just not about you or me.

The hope is that you find things here that will encourage and challenge you to get in the middle of change—not experiments or alternatives, but real change in your practice. And if none of this connects with you or if you seriously don't see the need, this was provided for you first, at the beginning. So you have the choice to read no further. However, if it does connect with you, read on.

May we be the generation of educators remembered as the one that finally did what had to be done, across the state, through every campus, and into each classroom. That's historic and we should be part of it.

INTRODUCTION

Peering Over the Edge

This book is not meant to be another book on how, where, or why education is lacking. Rather, this book is about systems. And when we discuss our education system, it's impossible to do so without pointing out why it's important to change that system. It's not meant to be an indictment on teaching or teachers. There is a true calling in genuine teachers and it demands a level of respect from all of us. Teachers are our greatest hope.

This book has been written with some projections, along with some risks, to state that:

- Change in education has already happened, but without realistic or broad implementation, and there doesn't seem to be any real effort to create a systemic implementation in any form beyond isolated pockets and alternative options.
- We are in danger of creating an "education reform" model adorned with computers and nice technology that doesn't actually disrupt practice, but merely supports the traditional teaching system.[1]
- There is a clear distinction between teaching systems that teach something and learning systems where students learn something.

- We have teaching systems created in the last century that have successfully controlled education so effectively that we now believe that this is how people learn.
- We will move to full-scale student-centered learning systems and educators unable to make the shift can, and will, be left behind.
- Our current state in education is composed of three basic systems (paradigms) identified as a teaching system that can't respond to each learner, further exacerbated by a testing system that doesn't provide effective measurement, and an honest education reform system characterized by small experiments and pockets of promise that delay broad systemic transformation.
- What will eventually break the industrial system[2] will be the consuming digital generations that will not tolerate the old system any longer.
- The one nonnegotiable item is that the system must experience transformative systemic change on a national scale that changes classroom practice in order to create sustainability in a world with emerging and expanding twenty-first-century resources.

Let's look at the three basic systems in education that should be addressed. First is the teaching system that forms the foundation for the way we've educated children in this country in our most recent history. It has a historical beginning, a mid-period when the concept of education reform was created, and is approaching systemic end.

The second system is the testing system, which was created during the period of education reform to address concerns related to measurement of the teaching system. This system controls so much of what we do now and isn't addressing our greatest needs related to measuring learning.

Lastly we have the education reform system. In the mid-1980s,[3] when we realized something had to be done, we responded with a genuine effort to address the issues. And we did the best we could. But we were not about to jump off a cliff. Any change or innovation would have to understand that the foundational structure of our teaching system wasn't going to be put at risk by any new idea.

So we tried out the latest experiments. We added new rooms to the house, but we were not about to remove the foundation of the structure. We had institutionalized the industrial teaching system and claimed it had ancient and revered status. This is how learners learn. So we could try out any new idea, test any new waters, and experiment away. But changing the foundation? Changing the paradigm? It just wasn't going to happen. It was too risky. And education reformers, some of the brightest minds we have, find it difficult when they push too hard.

While our system of education is a true teaching system, we struggle with the growing realization that learners are disconnecting. And in a teaching system, it's just best to blame the learner and throw money at the visible social, environmental, and economic issues the learner experiences.

So we spend countless dollars to improve the learner's state so that we can somehow improve the chances for academic success. Then when we don't get the results, we can more easily blame the learner for being disengaged and disconnected, and we can more easily absolve ourselves of one hard truth: it's our fault. First we have to qualify that statement.

Improving the state of the learner isn't bad. Yet once we make those improvements, we believe we can slide the learner back into the teaching system and everything will be fine. It's not true. *The primary issue we have to address is that we must begin a systemic and public strategy to draw a clear distinction between a teaching system and a learning system.*

Once we understand how to recognize and identify a teaching system (and understand why it has a short shelf life for the future) and understand how to recognize and identify a learning system (and launch the plan to change all education systemically), there will no longer be the need for the testing system and our trust in the learning system without the testing system can be a reality.

Most of the things you find here come from the viewpoint of an educational architect. There is often a disconnect between the research and the reality. Tremendous research informs us and presents what we need to do. Practitioners in the field know change is needed. Yet the reality is too real, so there is a fallback position that leans on teacher preparation and certification that has not kept pace with twenty-first-century needs. We are still training the way we trained. The need for educational architects, those who understand both the research and the practice, is great.

What is projected here is an observation of where we are and where we should go in education. It's not meant to be an intriguing idea or a proposal to consider. We've done that long enough and it has marginalized, isolated, or eliminated every attempt to reshape education for years.

Rather than just considering the idea of transformation, we should start laying out the plan. We've had thirty years of education reform. And those experienced as true reformers can be poised to lead us through that transformation. We can break away from the experimental laboratories and bring change into every classroom, for every child, by leveraging these tools for the transformation. We have the intelligence. We just need to match that intelligence with the will to do it for those generations of students to come.

NOTES

1. C. Christensen, C. W. Johnson, and M. B. Horn, *Disrupting Class: How Disruptive Innovation Will Change the Way the World Learns* (New York: McGraw-Hill, 2008).

2. Sir Ken Robinson, "Bring on the Learning Revolution," *Ted Talk*, 14:30; "We have to go from what is essentially an industrial model of education, a manufacturing model, which is based on linearity and conformity and batching people. We have to move to a model that is based more on principles of agriculture. We have to recognize that human flourishing is not a mechanical process; it's an organic process. And you cannot predict the outcome of human development. All you can do, like a farmer, is create the conditions under which they will begin to flourish."

3. United States National Commission on Excellence in Education, *A Nation at Risk: The Imperative for Educational Reform: A Report to the Nation and the Secretary of Education, United States Department of Education* (Washington, DC: Commission on Excellence in Education, 1983).

Chapter 1

WHY WE HAVE TO GET OVER OURSELVES

DOC'S STORY: "THE DEATH OF THE MOUSE"

She was obviously frustrated. It's sort of easy to know when this particular grandchild is frustrated. You can be watching football on Thanksgiving Day and try to ignore those small cries of annoyance, barely perceptible at first, yet increasing in volume each time. Try to ignore, keep watching the game. But, finally, her frustration seems to be on the verge of turning into tears. No granddad can ignore that. The child is clearly vexed. Get up and see what's going on.

I wander into the kitchen where our computer sits in an office area. What's wrong? Her mother quietly explains the problem. "She's not used to using a mouse for that program."

My preschool grandchildren use an online learning program at home. It's an amazing, engaging program, making learning fun and accessible for preschoolers. They love it. Here's the problem . . . they use it on their parents' handheld devices. Guess what? No mouse. It's all touchscreen. No mouse. These preschoolers swipe through the learning program with the tips of their fingers.

My granddaughter, as brilliant as she may be, was sitting there swiping away on the computer screen of my large desktop computer. And no matter how delicately she moved those fingers, that image on that screen never moved. Never responded. And she couldn't understand why Doc and BB's computer was so broken.

She's four. And we bought that desktop computer less than a year ago. Her mother had to sit down with her and patiently teach her how to use a mouse. Not because a mouse is the latest thing, but because the mouse is becoming a relic.

So to be clear, there were no mice living in our house when I was four. Any mice we saw were soon to be expired rodents that caused panic in my mom. And when computers became mainstream many years later, I liked the name of that handy tool that could move a cursor. That computer "mouse" was new and cool. Technology at its best.

Now here I sit, in my own kitchen on Thanksgiving Day, having to explain to my granddaughter what that prehistoric hand-thing is that she has to use to make her program work. And I'm hit with the fact that I'm on a fast-moving train to "obsolete town" where mice and old professors go to swap stories about the good old days. My irrelevancy is now in danger of skipping exponentially into a future where I can do what I need to do to remain significant or just sit on a bench and let it roll on without me.

I reach down and pet that old, dead mouse as it lay there on its mouse pad, silent in the glow of my computer screen. He had a good run.

Why is it important to even read or consider this book or the ideas presented here? We do not need another book on education reform. You will not have any revelations while reading this. There will be no enlightening instant when suddenly everything becomes clear and you're changed forever. There are no hidden secrets, no exposed conspiracy theories, and no earth-shattering news found in these pages. We do not need another book on education reform.

Books are written and read on education reform every day. Titles abound and shelves are full. A simple search will offer endless lists of books, videos, papers, and articles on reforming education. Excellent resources, expensive conferences, and exceptional PowerPoint presentations have been telling us we have to change for years. This is already out there.

So why write it? Simply this: *education reform has taken on a life of its own*. The reform industry has grown as large as the education industry. And the element of education reform is now an expectation. There is now a certainty of finding a reform piece in every district or state.

Courses and classes tell us and teach us that we have to reform. Yet we keep the train of traditional education practice rolling down a track made of bent and buckled iron.

In our effort to be everything for everyone, we've constructed a paradigm at the beginning of this century that is comfortable, while giving the appearance of being creative. We've reacted to our failures by constructing a paradigm that is acceptable, while giving the appearance of being revolutionary. Yet the train keeps rolling.

We do not change. And we don't have to change if we are happy with the contorted metal track. We have repaired and maintained this track for years. We know how to prevent a derailment. So if the trip can still happen for the rider, if they can still get there, if the walk across the stage to be handed a diploma can still occur, why change?

It's probably best to qualify the language. This book is not about education reform. In fact, the fear is that education reformers may be offended. Having dedicated our lives to the idea that we are the solution, we won't necessarily want to consider that we might be part of the problem. So it's important to construct, deconstruct, shape, and reshape the paradigm. In fact, we need to know what paradigms we should even address.

CLARIFYING THE LANGUAGE

Again, this is not a book about education reform. We need to shift who we are and change the paradigm of what we have to be going forward. We have to commit a full-on frontal attack on what actually needs to change. We have to reshape the paradigms of "teaching" and "learning." *We have to transform.* Starting with every classroom, our knowledge base has to shift.

"Reform": to improve something. "Transform": to change something completely. It may appear that the pieces of alternative options that everyone seems to have lying in a corner of the district, lined up on tables at the back of the classroom, or located in countless communities of the state are enough. They're not. We have to change how we think about the essence of the system. It doesn't need to be reformed. It needs a transformation. It's not a broken track or just a twisted one that can still deliver, but at what cost?

The problem may be that we need to "nuance" the language, the understanding, and the agreements. We should start calling ourselves "education transformers." We should use transformation rather than reform every time. And we should do this across the board, nationally. We should change what we mean when we think about teaching, change what we mean when we think about learning, and accept nothing less than a transformation of the entire system.

If we're considering any kind of transformation, such as the one being presented, we have to ask ourselves why it's even important. One can find reasons everywhere. The primary reasons are easily offered and discussed often. To narrow it down to any one reason could be a simple process, except for the fact that the specific *one reason* often just depends on who you're talking to and what their interests may be related to the issue at any given time.

This book, though, will not address the *idea* of change. Rather, it calls for the *implementation* of change. And because we are discussing a disruptive[1] *implementation* rather than a disruptive *idea*, we can end up, as typically happens, thinking a lot about this but not doing much at all. And because the education community seems willing to discuss anything related to education reform, this book could end up being just another one in the pile. In education, we like to be involved in thought-provoking dialogue. We want to be known as a community of thinkers, people who are open and willing to think and consider new ideas.

Consider this, though, as you read. Consider the term *thought provoking*. As you turn the pages, know that the focus for what's written here has an intentional and measurable end. Rather than seeing the word *thought* in that term, zero in on the word *provoke*. To challenge, stir up, arouse, and call forth. Often the word is used in a negative sense as one who is provoking you or stirring up emotions of anger or feelings.

When you're provoked, someone has done something or said something that stirs and produces feelings in you. Too many times in education, we focus on the "thought" in *thought provoking* and settle for that. Think about this and give some thought to that. And everything stays as it is because we never get past the "thought."

In this book, we want to move beyond just the thinking. And maybe we need to be provoked. The primary idea we have to understand is that *implementation trumps intent every time*. We know so much but do so little sometimes. So we like to have our thinking provoked.

We never turn down opportunities to have our thinking provoked. We think about it. We analyze it. And in the world of education reform, being provoked is a given, as long as we're only talking about "thought"-provoking ideas. Even as we *think* about the things presented, we can be sincere and genuine in our *thinking*.

But again, implementation trumps intent every time. There are two ways to approach the thinking when presented with ideas that can be disruptive. We can spend our time thinking about all the reasons why it won't work and all the ways it will fail. "You just don't know our kids. We appreciate everything you've said, but a little explanation might help you see why what you're talking about just won't work here."

Or we can spend our time thinking about how we can make it work. We see the difficulties and we know the problems that might have to be addressed. But if we know the ideas are nonnegotiable and the work has to be done, we exert much more effort into actually doing something to make it happen.

We can think all we want, but it's only the doing that will count. We can know everything, but if that knowing never actually changes anything, we are a community of great thinkers. Given some space we could do more, but we can't because we've already told you why it won't work. We give a cursory pat on the head to those who brought the idea to the table. It was a good try.

This book isn't written to just be thought provoking. Implementation trumps intent and whatever we think to do, or intend to do, is great, but it means nothing if we don't actually do it. We have thousands of people attending our conferences and taking notes. The greatest weapon in our toolbox is the Power Point. But if we leave the conference with a lot of intent and return to our campus with no implementation, our points have no power.

So know this as you read: this is not a simplistic, manipulative attempt to stir up anyone. It's not someone just saying something harsh or offensive just to get a rise out of people. Those attempts would be prideful and would certainly deserve any indifference they would receive from an intelligent audience.

But this is certainly an attempt to provoke. We should always appreciate the thinking. And in education reform, we should be consistently impressed with those among us who have proven to be our best thinkers and our greatest minds. We shouldn't venture to the other end of that spectrum, believing that it's only the doers that count.

We need the thinking, but we've turned thinking about change into an art. We've developed this thinking into a skill where we delay, buy more time, and hold off any real change until things cool off enough and the pressure to actually implement systemic change goes back to the end of the line, safe for another year.

THE CURRENT SYSTEMS

The current system of education, institutionalized during the last century and hanging on into this century, is not financially, organizationally, or intellectually sustainable for too much longer. No matter what we may currently accept about innovation or change, we always seem to be building a fence around that traditional system of teaching that prevents any new idea from actually changing the way we educate. The teaching system is institutionalized still.

Sustainability into our future is, and should be, our goal in education. The very idea of education is to pass knowledge to next generations in order to ensure a healthy society going forward. The system employed in the last century, and hanging around at the outset of this one, is not sustainable.

The populations of students are not shrinking. There are more learners than ever before and this isn't changing. The industrial system is created within strict confines and depends on availability of resources that will not have the capacity to keep up in the future. Infrastructure and personnel that can fit within the confined structural boundaries will not keep pace with the growing numbers of students.

Financial demands will not be able to continue at the current growth needed if transformative change doesn't happen. Smaller communities, no longer able to afford their own schools due to the smaller student population and increasing financial burdens, will find their entire identity dramatically changed or eliminated as they are forced to consolidate with surrounding small community schools. Or worse, their students will be swallowed up by consolidation with large urban or suburban schools. The small town community defined by its pride in its hometown school could become a thing of the past.[2]

Digital natives,[3] so called because of their birth into or during an age when digital technology invaded and conquered our land, are graduating into, and out of, our colleges and universities, ready to take their place in society as competitive and competent adults. These learners have benefited from a background inundated with the advancement of a digital world that keeps it fresh, engaging, and changing, so much so that change has become an expected and normal perspective of almost everything.

If it isn't changing, if it isn't getting better, if the upgrade is too slow in coming, the digital native immediately moves on to the next biggest thing. Not only does someone create it, but there is an immediate and urgent demand to begin changing and improving it as soon as it hits the street. In fact, changing it, improving it, and reforming it are, at the very least, just as important as the original genesis of the idea. The upgrading component of digital is a formidable industry.

No longer are we, or they, satisfied to buy the new thing and adjust to it, learn how to navigate the glitches and bugs, or work around the parts of it that just don't work quite right. We expect the creators to see the glitches, know that we see the glitches, and also know that we will move on and find another creator if the upgrade doesn't address those glitches within a month.

We've replaced "bells and whistles" with "bugs and whistles." We have something we want to do, follow, or just have on our phone. So we search. Now this isn't some scavenger hunt or seeking of treasure that takes a lot of our time or effort. It only involves typing into a "window" on the home page of a search engine.

When we push "enter," anything remotely connected to those words we typed pops up in front of us, listed according to rather specific criteria. And the bold title followed by some nonbold sentences gives us clues and previews of what awaits us if we are interested. Simply by placing our cursor on that bold print, which turns our cursor into a hand pointing at that title, we can click and the world opens up.

THE "WHAT IF . . ."

So let's throw that entire process back to 1975 and put the twenty-first-century twist on it. You need a new pair of boots. So you reach for your keys to drive thirty miles to the boot store. Oh wait, you don't have to drive there. There are several boot stores in your living room.

You walk into the living room and begin the process of walking down the aisles of all the stores that have now expanded the size of the room. Oh wait, you don't have to spend your time walking down those aisles. You can just sit down in your chair and let those stores roll slowly by and spend your time choosing which one you want to explore.

Now as they roll by, you suddenly realize that if you want to truly decide which one you want to see, you'll have to get up and look on the shelves. Oh wait, you don't have to get up. All you have to do is point at the storefront and an employee of that particular store will step right up and inquire as to which shelf you'd like to see.

So you choose a store, point, and the dutiful employee comes to your aid. He asks specific questions about the exact sort of boot you're looking for. Well, that's a little tough. You like brown boots with a traditional toe. But you already have a pair like that, so maybe you'll go with black this time. Wait, you remember catching a brief glance of a cool-looking pair of brown/black boots when the shelf rolled by. Maybe that one. "Why don't you just bring me several pairs of boots? I'm just not sure and I hope it's not too much trouble."

The employee doesn't even give you a dirty look. He immediately runs down the aisle, pulling several boots from the shelves. In fact, he seems to intuitively know the exact options in boots that would appeal to you. He lays them out, with the one he thinks would probably be the perfect pair placed first. You don't like those.

He then puts that pair out of the way and, one by one, he brings out each pair, giving you time to carefully inspect each choice. In fact, you sort of like the third pair and spend a lot of time looking it up and down and inspecting it for a while. However, something just seems to hold you back. You work your way through ten pairs of boots. You get to the end of the group he brought. You've taken quite a lot of his precious time, but not once does he ever complain or act impatient.

You then spring it on him. "By the way, sir. I don't have any money on me right now. In fact, sir, I never really intended to buy any boots from you today. I just had a few minutes and wanted to look at new boots I couldn't afford. Hope you don't mind putting those back on the shelves for me. Now that I think about it, I liked three of the pairs you brought me. Would you mind holding those back for me? I just want to come back and look at them sometimes. Now, I won't have money then either. But, I do want to visit them from time to time. Just to see what I'm going to buy someday. Oh and when you get all these back on the shelf for me, would you please get out of my living room?"

Silly, isn't it? Nowhere in 1975 could that, or would that, have happened. But the reason it seems so silly now is because of the fundamental change that occurred between then and now. This very process is common now. Not only does it happen, it happens every day, all day long. In fact, this silly illustration can't even come close to truly showing how incredibly convenient and accessible things like this are now. It's a strange world. But it's only strange if we, especially those of us known as digital immigrants, refuse to give all we can to understand it and live in it.

But the digital native was born in this world. They are growing up in it. And as strange as this world may be now, imagine how much stranger it will get. So stand in front of the train, but that won't stop it from rolling down that track. Why not jump on?

It's true that not all progress is good. Just because it's new doesn't mean it's something great. But this is, as long as we draw some clear distinctions between those changes we should embrace and those things we should protect. Protecting a teaching system that cannot do what we need to do for learners has to stop. It needs to go away.

Hopefully, we can get to where we should be while getting everybody on board to make the trip with us. As for those who believe we shouldn't make the trip at all? In our very near future, we may find no room for them. Let's be honest. No one is ever saying that we should rewrite history, abandon classical content, or change the bedrock truths that we've always taught. But how we educate should, can, and will change.

We already have multiple and increasing problems with the traditional industrial teaching system of education. These problems already exist and the system hasn't been able to effectively address or resolve them within its confinement. To be sustainable, our educational system must be transformed and structured in a way that can adequately meet the demands and resolve the identified problems that already exist.

In fact, some will say that writing another book on change is unnecessary because we already have many books on change. Yet even this argument becomes one of the fundamental flaws we now face. We believe that we are changing. And that seems to be enough for now. Yet *a serious systemic transformation that replaces the teaching system is not occurring.*

Technology has already changed our world. Educational systems will change. There will be fights, arguments, and barriers. However, barriers, through common sense and rising demands, will eventually become mere bumps. While most elements of our society welcomed and embraced the advantages and benefits of how technology could improve what they do, education, entrenched in a teaching-centric system, wasted much on trying to convince, scare, or intellectualize us into believing that the benefits would not improve learning.

Though we will see much more about the difference between a teaching system and a learning system later, the arguments against technology possessed some merit simply because those making expensive decisions on deployment were forcing learning tools into a teaching system that won't support the capacity and potential of twenty-first-century tools. However, all this will change. The educational system will transform and will become all it should be. The question becomes: *Which generation of educators will finally take the risks and challenges to truly create and implement the twenty-first-century system?*

Students are smarter than we think. As educators, we should reflect on the intelligence of our students. It's interesting to ask teachers who they think is the smartest in the room. What would happen if we told teachers that we had changed our hiring system? What if we told them that tomorrow they will be given the exit-level state-mandated algebra test that is given to high school students, and that based on their ability to pass or fail the test, we will decide if they have a job or not?

If they fail, they will not have a job. If enough of them fail, we will close their campus. Not only will they lose their job, we will also call their parents and inform them that their child is a failure. How many are willing to take that kind of high-stakes test? Yet it would be good to remind them that those students in their classrooms will be doing that exact thing this year.

What's interesting is that there are some who will argue that it's not a level playing field because those students will have plenty of time to prepare for the test. Agreed. So how much time would it take? How much time do we need to get to the same level as those students? This leads to a question that has to be asked: *Why do we continue to do to students what we ourselves, as adults, would most likely take someone to court over?*

Students are smart. They know how to learn material and content. In a teacher-centric educational system, *they know how to learn a teacher*. Not only are they capable of so much learning, they've also grown up in a technology-rich world. These digital natives know so much more than we do. They swipe away and move through technology in every area of life. Any system that depends on consumer engagement as much as education does will not be sustainable once the consumer matures to a point of intolerance and if that system continues to ignore the demand for transformation. The system will change.

UNDERSTANDING THE DEVELOPMENT OF THE SYSTEM

The current industrial system is not the ancient model of education or the near past model. It is the model created for the industrial period. It is not the evolved perfect model at the apex of an evolved framework of perfection. It's an isolated model created during the industrial period that used the best of the industrialized elements for an isolated period of time and need. All industries have intelligently *transformed*, rather than evolved, to remain current and relevant, except for education.

One needs only to look at how we created this system to begin to understand how we got here. When organizing the model for schooling, our nation followed the examples and created systems of men who were well known for developing successful models that organized factories, bureaucracies, and industrial processes. Some, like Frederick Taylor and Max Weber, were known for things far removed from a classroom. These were all great men and we needed, at that point in our growth as a nation, whatever we could learn from them.

Break the year into a predetermined "first day to last day" of school, decide how much and exactly what a child should learn between those two significant days, divide that content into well-paced segments equally separated into six-week or nine-week sections, further break it down into week-long sections, then day-long sections, then finally give each subject area an amount of time each day for kids to concentrate on each equally.

Bring the students in, have them focus on a subject for that determined number of minutes during the day, then ring a bell that tells them to stop thinking about that, go to the next section, and think about another subject for the same number of minutes. If everybody behaves and just follows the flow, the subject gets covered for that day, that week, that six-week period, and, in the end, for the entire year. Do it right and the student gets a fair and equal presentation of every subject during the school year.

As we moved into and through the industrialized way of life, this system of education served its purpose. Around the middle of the twentieth century, there began to be calls for personalized education. However, trying to fit personalization in the middle of a teacher-centric system is impossible. So anything that didn't follow the rules of the industrialized model was considered *alternative.* That has been a successful deflection for years.

It's been so successful that even though the very people responsible for the decisions admit that change is necessary, we continue to draw specific and immovable boundaries around any genuine change and call it reform. *We don't actually touch the system.*

In that system, it becomes very easy to blame anybody and everybody, depending on the context of our discussion at the time. It's become too easy to blame the student, the teacher, the parent, administration, policymakers, the government, and everyone else.

The problem is that all of these are to blame and none of these are to blame. *The entire blame lies with the system.* The system is an all-consuming cultural umbrella, a belief system that encompasses every approach, idea, and understanding we have about education in America. We should love educators. We should not blame educators unless they defend the system. Anyone who can continue defending a system that is broken gets in the way.

We planned and established (adopted) a system, a way of schooling, in our country. The problem is that we began believing that our teaching system is actually a learning system. We began saying that this is how people learn instead of simply admitting that this is more about how we teach.

Therefore we believe that anything not fitting in that model is "alternative" and for "those kids," the ones who "don't get it." We moved the system from an adopted status to an accepted status, then to a nonnegotiable institutionalized status that demands that anything outside this framework is "alternative." And the nation bought into it. It has never been clearer than now, though, that we can definitively state that *this is not how we learn.*

We are supposed to learn. The saddest state is one in which a person, even an educator, refuses to learn. Learning creates change and good things come from learning. The best educators care much more about the learning process than the teaching process.

We are currently living in a new land of opportunity where the gold we seek lies just below the surface. This century offers opportunities for learners that have never existed before. We have to stop politicizing the advancement of technology and start leveraging what it can do for us.

Digital immigrants are typically in control of how we deploy technology. Students, digital natives, were born into a world that is infused with technology and it's a natural part of their life. They wait for us to get over ourselves.

Future historical records will most likely note that we, as adults, wasted a lot of time getting to a comfort level where we could trust these strange new inventions simply because they weren't around when we went to school. Make no mistake, technology can do some things for good educational practice that a teacher cannot do. So to even spend much more time debating the need to form an aggressive plan to utilize technology in a disruptive and systemic way to transform our entire educational frontier is wasted time.

NAVIGATING THE CHANGE

So we have problems. Rather than taking a negative "here's what's wrong" approach, this book is meant to hopefully be an architectural drawing, a positive and proactive direction, starting with the very idea that what we have is a problem. I think the better idea is that we have equations.

Our challenge lies in the immediate future. It's not a problem that has an easy answer, or even one single answer; it's an equation that has different ingredients, formulas, and pieces. We have practitioners and researchers. *What we need right now, in this generation of educators, are architects.*

Knowing that, this book is written to be more than theory. There are better books you can read focused on the theory, the "why" we do what we do. This book is also written to be more than a step-by-step manual. You can find plenty of manuals, usually sold off the back of bandwagons, that take you through each step to implement the latest program. Theory gives us knowledge and understanding, but it doesn't change anything. Manuals change everything until the next manual is published.

We can know and understand everything, but that doesn't mean our knowledge causes sustainable change. We can also be champions of change that keep looking around for the perfect answer, implementing the newest and the best, until something newer and better distracts us.

Students need empowerment. Students need advocacy. Students need shepherding. These may not be comfortable terms or concepts for educators. They certainly seem to mean different things to different people. For the sake of this book, however, we should see these concepts as aligned within a framework of systemic transformation for our classrooms and campuses.

Empowerment, the idea of giving your power away, is tricky and risky. We have authority and power in our classrooms. As the teacher, we can speak with power or we can speak with authority. These two are not the same.

EMPOWERING THE STUDENT

Power can be intimidating. When one speaks with power, it implies control and demand. In many scenarios, this is necessary. We need powerful leaders. We even need those leaders to control these scenarios. Think military engagements, legal proceedings, and tension-filled environments, where the right decisions have to be made to ensure the best outcome. Our classrooms, however, are not these environments. We will have to empower learners.

Empowerment means one thing throughout this book: *self-directed learning*. Consider this equation: giving freedom to the student within the classroom (an expectation for the learner) plus taking responsibility for learning by the student (an expectation from the learner) equals empowerment.

Many might believe that we do empower students. But a systemic empowerment, a mandated pedagogical practice that hands over the decision making and creates a self-directed learning experience, isn't happening.

Many might believe we can't empower students. The fear is that they cannot be trusted and it creates a serious trap that they fall into quickly, digging themselves a hole too deep to escape. In so many of our "pockets of promise" experiments and our better classrooms, that trust has already been given and the results have proven that the trust is well placed.

Many might believe we can only empower certain students, types of students, or portions of our classroom. That excuse has been allowed to strengthen itself through the years of teacher-centric education and it is supposed to, as it has, create a fear among us. Yet in a learning system where the teacher has the capacity to engage with each student, any learner can, will, and does respond effectively.

All of us, including teachers and parents, want to be empowered in our life. We need to have the level of our responsibility to make things happen equal our level of authority to make those things happen. Why do we deny that to our learners?

The answer to that question is the very reason we have to transform education. Most likely, the reason we might deny empowerment is because students are younger than we are. They haven't reached a level of understanding in their growth and maturity. Therefore, we cannot empower them. Yet the position should be that if we are to teach anything, we should teach them these things. They should learn wisdom and responsibility from us.

Yet how many of our students actually learn any of this from our teaching systems? They learn obedience. They learn compliance. They become reluctant learners. Not all of them. Some are granted certain levels of empowerment and have preferred status. Some react badly and we tighten the screws.

Too often, we become compliance officers. Our classroom can become a bureaucracy existing within a campus bureaucracy existing within a district bureaucracy existing within a state bureaucracy existing within a national bureaucracy. That bureaucracy exists for public, private, and charter schools. At the end of the day, it's only the kid that matters. *We have to empower twenty-first-century students and create self-directed learning as the pedagogical foundation for each and every learner.*

ADVOCACY

Students need advocacy. The term can often be hijacked as meaning that we should be trying to meet every social and environmental need. While that's certainly not disputed here, advocacy, for our purposes, primarily refers to anything that motivates and provides support for a learner to be engaged with the learning process.

What keeps that student engaged? Some students stay engaged because they have a high sense of ambition, goals, and intrinsic motivation. Some stay in the middle of their studies because they want to play football. Maybe the student has a highly engaged parent or a teacher who pulls alongside the student and provides support. Or maybe the student is popular or pretty.

Advocacy is necessary. Those adults who give themselves to students every day need the time and the capacity to advocate for every student, every day. Yet a teaching system robs those adults of the opportunity to engage with each student personally.

Teachers should shepherd their students. The term *shepherd* is another unusual term for what we do in our classrooms. However, this is the simplest, yet most profound, element of good teaching. Shepherding is characterized by the process of teaching wisdom to our kids. And the teaching system doesn't allow us to shepherd many.

It's time to become architects, designers and builders of houses that withstand any storm. Our theory must meet our practice. Our knowledge must inform our work. And our work must be created to last.

Hopefully, this book will serve as an architectural drawing. Rather than saying, "try this and see how this works," what you'll find here is an urgent call to look at the systemic change we have to make that transforms the structure and the foundation of how we educate. *We need to consider how we can stop doing experimental labs and create an entire transformation, one that changes the classroom, the campus, the district, charters, and private schools. In other words, the way we educate nationwide.*

Architects consider each aspect of a design. Every component of the structure is analyzed. Every architect understands there are nonnegotiable things that must be present and cannot be betrayed if the creation is to be sustainable into the future. It's important to know that we are discussing systemic practice, not content. The classical content, that body of knowledge founded by a liberal arts understanding and based on great literature and logic, remains as our scope.

We do, however, speak about pedagogy. How we pass on that knowledge to this and other generations is important.

When we had an industrialized way of life, we could demand that learners adjust to the model because we were limited by the available resources. In this century, we have so many choices and so many resources that we have to go beyond the paradigm of limited choice and begin a serious effort to develop the paradigm of educational architecture: architecture, designers, and creators that can pull in the available choices of resources to personalize and create self-directed learning opportunities. Each generation deserves it. And each learner can now have it. But we have to get over ourselves first.

SUMMARY THOUGHTS

- We need to move everything, our understanding, language, and practice, from education reform to an environment of transformation.
- Implementation (actually doing what we know to do) is the only verifiable proof that we believe in transformational change for twenty-first-century students.
- We must have a major shift in our paradigm about teaching and learning.
- Education architecture will be the most significant element for designing and resolving our learning environments.

NOTES

1. C. Christensen, C. W. Johnson, and M. B. Horn, *Disrupting Class: How Disruptive Innovation Will Change the Way the World Learns* (New York: McGraw-Hill, 2008).

2. D. Cooley and D. Floyd, "Small Rural School District Consolidation in Texas: An Analysis of Its Impact on Cost and Student Achievement," *Administrative Issues Journal: Education, Practice, and Research* 3, no. 1 (2013): 45–63.

3. M. Prensky, "Digital Natives, Digital Immigrants," *On the Horizon* 9, no. 5 (2001): 1–6.

Chapter 2

TEACHING OR LEARNING?

DOC'S STORY

I love my hometown. It was a small place, a population of only about 350 people, and it was the perfect place to grow up. My high school, like the majority of all schools, utilized the same learning system and the industrial organization style still used today. We reported for class when the bell told us to, paid attention to a subject for forty-five minutes, then dutifully packed up and headed to the next class when the bell told us to do so.

Together, we worked our way page by page, chapter by chapter through the textbook, trusting that those textbook publishers knew what was best for all of us. This was Americana education and if it was good enough for our parents and grandparents, it was certainly good enough for us.

One year, in one of my classes, we didn't actually get to everything in the book by the end of the year. We just didn't have time to cover it all. But that didn't matter because the rules were that every red-blooded child in America deserved the high school credit if they had served their time. So even though we didn't get to some of the information, I still received my high school credit.

The amazing thing is that my high school credit stands right beside the high school credit of any professor or researcher in America. Sure, they may conduct complex experiments and solve intellectual riddles that have puzzled man for centuries. They may cure disease and they may discover new frontiers. But if you slap their high school transcript up against mine, I have the same credentials they do in that high school course. I didn't cover all of it, but that doesn't matter in Americana education The final bell rang on the final day and I had done the time.

I've lived with a deep fear since that day that I'll be walking through the woods and I'll hear a low, menacing growl up ahead. Rounding a corner, I'll see it: a beast I've never seen before, never heard of before, or never even imagined existed before that day, some terrible mix of bear, cougar, and hog, all rolled into one wild beast that has one intent: to destroy me. This is no normal situation.

Had it been the usual wild animal, I would have known what to do. But this isn't the usual. This is something I've never known was even a part of this world. This must have been covered in the final pages of the textbook we never finished.

I loved my high school and I loved my teachers. What I don't love is the industrial system from 1973, 1954, and 2012 that still acts like we don't live in a new era. This is a new pioneer world of opportunity and we have to be smart enough to leverage every piece of it to transform our educational system.

Learning is a wonderful thing. Being given the opportunity to discover new things, making connections that we didn't know existed before, adding information to prior knowledge that helps us understand our world more clearly—all of this is learning and we grow as individuals because of it.

Our conventional system of education is founded upon a teaching system. While this served us well for years, the system has become a barrier to true innovation and responsiveness to today's learner. It has never been a learning system. It's a teaching system. It was created to organize schooling, to manage overwhelming numbers of children, to make sure every subject was covered equally, and to make sure that we adults could rest in the fact that we gave opportunity for all kids, all subjects, and all content equally and fairly.

But again, it's never been a learning system. It's always been a teaching system. And if our goal, our hope, and our intent is to provide a teaching system for our children, then we should say "well done." It's possible that no nation could have organized a better system. It's seriously a great factory model developed when a factory model was necessary and considered a dramatic improvement over what needed to be done for the sake of learners. We should be proud of the way we responded to the needs of our country during the industrial period when this style of addressing tremendous growth of possibilities was necessary.

What is most significant, though, is how we view the paradigm of this development. When we consider other industry growth and development in this country, we understand that the establishment of practice for these industries was created in response to the technological, bureaucratic, and current status of all possibilities for that specific time period in our history. We see the changes of those, even dramatic changes, as being natural and necessary.

Not so with education. We study the history of the development of the factory model school and pat ourselves on the back, rightfully so. However, we embedded the "idea" of our educational system into the minds of our nation so that the "picture" one creates of a classroom is a *human vocalizing and controlling content to an organized group of learners*. That's a paradigm, a way of thinking.

And because we institutionalized the paradigm, there is often a feeling that education gets a free pass when it comes to the dramatic transformation experienced by other industries. For other industries, we would never advocate practice that has clearly proven that its delivery system and measurement are outdated and ineffective in a modern era. Yet we continue to hang on to these very elements in education.

In a system wherein students can navigate the components, maybe even bypassing the most important aspects of learning, how many high school students today have achieved the Algebra I credit and are still unable to do Algebra? Kids are smart. They know how to adjust. They learn the teacher. And they know how to run the numbers.

Most teachers want the best for their students. They don't want to make a student repeat a grade level. That's a lot of pressure. Well-meaning adults allow all kinds of options to help kids get the grade: "show up for the school play and I'll give you ten points in the grade book," "redo that assignment you failed," "do this or do that and you'll get extra points." We see negotiated grades and students who know how to charm their way to a passing grade all the time.

It's not a matter of trying to simplify things here to the point of being ridiculous. Honestly, though, it can reach ridiculous at times. The single greatest mistake we make is when we state that our system of teaching is a learning system. It isn't. *This is not the way we learn*. Yet we have countless numbers of people, mostly educators, who call anything other than the factory industrial system of education "alternative."

Alternative to what? If you say it's "alternative," that's just edu-speak for something designed for the kids who just don't get it. *Oh, you're talking about those kids*. It's a negative connotation meant to diminish the most natural, most successful, and most logical approach we should have in our schools. It's protectionist, territorial, and damaging. It's meant to protect the teaching profession as we have designed it and expanded it in this nation.

But it's not sustainable into our future. We have to stop protecting this and reshape the paradigm so that the "picture" we see when we have the "thought" of education is only focused on learning.

GRADING

In a teaching system, grading is a big deal. The teacher assigns and then assesses. Teachers understand it. Kids understand it. Parents understand it. It's a comfortable part of the system. Everybody knows the rules. Learn the teacher and do what you have to do to make sure you're aware of the time limit and can be above that 70 percent line on the last day of school. Done. Credit granted and you don't have to worry about that course anymore. "What's my kid's grade?"

So what should we really be looking for when we talk about learning? Mastery, objective mastery, not subject to any argument or decision making on the part of a teacher. Learning is a progression of adding new knowledge to prior knowledge. In order to truly learn, one has to show mastery of content. If you are adding new knowledge, you must show mastery of prior knowledge.

A teaching system, well-organized but totally dependent on a timed, paced calendar, isn't suited for objective mastery. You can't have objective mastery if it's in the hands of subjective adults who have the massive responsibility of *giving grades*.

All students should be involved in mastery learning systems. In a mastery-based system, it's not the grade that matters. So what does matter? One word: progress. If you're in a mastery-based learning system, the only thing that matters is whether you are progressing. You can't go to next the level unless you master the level you're currently on.

Once you've mastered it, you're allowed to move on, even if you've mastered it in the middle of a school year and even if the student sitting beside you hasn't mastered it. Therefore instead of looking at grades, you're looking for progress. If you're progressing, you're "passing."

What is sufficient "passing" in a mastery-based learning system? Sadly, we have also institutionalized an acceptance of 70 percent as sufficient for this country. It's interesting to see how kids, coaches, parents, and doctoral students run the numbers all the time just to reach, or achieve, that 70 percent.

Why would 70 percent be enough, anywhere? If you truly master content objectively, you should score 90 percent before being given the privilege of moving to the next level of new knowledge. You should be able to prove that you know 90 percent of the current content before you're ready to add new content on top of that.

In this day of emerging technology, when learning is available and accessible twenty-four hours a day, we must respond appropriately. We've passed the days when we needed to control the timing and pace of exposure and introduction to content for learners. It's already out there and they know how to get it.

We have to start being aggressive in our response. Learners are different. Transforming the system of schooling in our nation is upon us and it won't suddenly disappear. In our very near future, when a parent asks, "How's my kid doing?" they won't be asking for the grade. They'll be asking for the progress.

Mastery-based learning should, and has to, become the bottom-line standard for everything we do when it comes to content learning. It's important. It's just facts and information, but that information should be learned. There has to be a foundation base of content that should be learned, and we cripple students when we stick it in an industrial assembly line system that subjects the learner to clocks and calendars.

Some kids have the cognitive capacity to learn this quickly and easily, but the clock and the calendar keep them on schedule with everybody else. You can't get your credit in February. What on earth will you do in March? Heaven forbid you finish that course in December because the state won't let you take your state assessment until April.

Some kids need a little more time and opportunities to learn it, but they have to stay up with everybody else. The end of the semester is coming and we have to keep up. So even though they could succeed with the time and opportunity, the clock and the calendar keep moving and it doesn't matter if you didn't get to go deep enough to really learn. Just get enough of it to pass the test. You won't actually remember much of it later, but it doesn't matter. You had the grade on the last day. The majority of kids just learn the system, its clocks and its calendars.

The concepts of grading, progress, and mastering those things we should learn will be important as we transform from a teaching system to a learning system. There are other important elements of a teaching system that must be challenged as well. One significant element is that of personalization. Though all of us are individuals, different in so many ways, a teaching system demands that we fit ourselves within the confines of the teaching environment. Most learners have the capacity, or advocacy, to do this.

THE SERIOUS SIDE OF DISENGAGEMENT

The growing number of students dropping out or disengaging from the learning process informs us that we are graduating or losing so many adolescents who have developed, or are developing, an interesting perception about themselves: helplessness. To be helpless is to have the inability to help yourself; to be weak or powerless. Helplessness is a belief system, a condition whereby one believes that he or she cannot help him- or herself, he or she is powerless to do anything to improve his or her position, and it produces a resignation to one's fate.

Helplessness can become a lifestyle that controls every aspect of your life, so much so that even when your circumstances could change and, with a little effort, everything could improve and be better for you, you don't have the inner strength or confidence to do those things to make it happen. Helplessness is a product of being disenfranchised, robbed of the opportunities that can increase your capacity and belief in having the ability to change your situation.

Can we "teach" people to be helpless? Can we place them in systems that divide, separate, and choose for them who they are, what they can be, and what they can't be? Can systems that we force on people make their decisions for them at an early age and be so overwhelming that it informs their development as a person and instills in them a belief system that makes them suffer from helplessness? Is there such a condition as "learned" helplessness (focus on the word *learned*)?[1]

We should highly regard those who study the human condition and help us understand how and why people function and relate to the world around them. Some studies have shown that, particularly with animal subjects, if that subject were placed in an unacceptable situation for an extended period of time, even when the unacceptable elements of the situation were later removed, the subject would not make the effort or perform the actions necessary to improve or change their personal circumstances.

The subjects had *learned to be helpless*, that they could do nothing to change their situation. They no longer blamed the unacceptable elements for their plight; they instead believed they were helpless, no matter what. They suffered from "learned helplessness."

Can we "teach" people to be helpless if we place them in unacceptable situations that can disenfranchise them, rob them of the opportunity to develop as a learner with the capacity to learn more and do more? Could that be one of the reasons why we see more and more students disengaging from an educational process? Why our numbers of dropouts keep increasing? Why even the ones who remain in our classrooms eventually disengage from the process? Why learning loses its excitement and creative potential in a learner?

The current institutionalized practice of the current system of education is a teaching system that cannot meet the demands of the twenty-first century if it refuses to change or transform into a system that can leverage all we have available to us now. Teaching systems teach and do it well. That does not mean learners learn.

It has become very easy to blame everybody and everything else. At the end of the day, it doesn't matter. Our students become victims of learned helplessness and our future could be filled with generations and entire layers of society that have learned that they are helpless and will walk through life being helpless because that's what they believe about themselves. Conditioning from an early age of life is hard to change.

TESTING OUR COMFORT LEVEL

We are too uncomfortable with the idea that every person has the potential to succeed. It's interesting to ask teachers what would happen if everyone in the class received an "A." When asked this, they get uncomfortable, knowing that their principal will probably schedule a meeting with them. Why? To throw a party? To hand that teacher a trophy? To congratulate that educator for being the consummate teacher?

Probably not. They don't see that as being the outcome of the meeting. The principal wants to meet with them to discover what went wrong. To find at what point they dropped their standards, made everything so easy that everybody could pass. To uncover their lack of ability to be a real teacher. The paradigm is that, if you're a real teacher, there will be no way that everyone can succeed.

The idea is uncomfortable and flies in the face of good education in this country. We even do it at high levels. When too many students succeed on state testing, well, it must be because we've made the test too easy. So we change it, pay huge amounts of money for huge numbers of professionals to design test questions that will trip them up, all under the umbrella of critical thinking. We cannot have everyone passing. We can even assign percentages of expected failures for every class or teacher. If everyone succeeds, it's too uncomfortable.

A teaching system requires that we have a comfortable percentage of failures to prove that we are actually teaching. A testing system requires we have an acceptable percentage of passers. There's a happy medium we shoot for every year. It's as if each school year has become a "season," a competitive game of numbers. No one sees the billboard at the city limits stating victory because the district only had 18 percent of their children fail last year. Yet we find the banners and billboards (like trophies from last season) stating the "championship season" we had last year when 82 percent of our children sufficiently passed at game time.

A system designed around the teaching process will always focus on the wrong thing in the twenty-first century. Teaching large numbers of learners, where every learner is paced to the group, and the pace demands every learner's compliancy to the system, produces a certain number of failures. We are comfortable with that because it means we taught. The testing system serves as a way of making sure we don't carry this idea to the extreme. Somewhere in the middle of it all sits a kid that needs that teacher, that adult.

Though we may have had the excuse of not being able to expect a human teacher to differentiate between every learner in the past, we no longer have that luxury. Students who have the cognitive capacity to accelerate their learning have the right to be involved in a learning system that allows them to do that, instead of being frustrated with a paced system that slows them up and holds them back. Why should we care? Only if we need to make sure it's managed and the teaching is organized in our comfortable classroom. Let too many of them get ahead and it becomes unmanageable and the organized lesson plan can just be thrown out the window.

Students who have need of additional assistance to succeed have the right to be involved in a learning system that allows them to receive that, instead of being frustrated with a paced system that keeps moving forward, leaving them behind. They deserve the engagement of educators without relegating them to an "alternative" status. Educators need to be engaged with them. But we have to finish the chapter, finish the section, and finish the book.

What of those in the middle? They have learned to keep the pace, navigate the system, and learn the teacher. That's not engagement with the learning process.

In this age of new learners, we have the potential to focus our efforts on individuals in every classroom. Our answers for this equation do not rest merely with technology. Technology is a tool that must be leveraged to improve our capacity to personalize learning. Therein lies the ability, finally, to diagnose and prescribe rigorous opportunities for every child. The arguments for technology in our schools have been stated and the significance has already been realized.[2] Two cautions regarding this must be stated as well.

APPROACHING TECHNOLOGY APPROPRIATELY

First, technology does not replace the teacher. Though we have employed a teaching system, and therefore defined teaching by and through that system in the last century, we have now progressed to acknowledge that we must transform to a learning system. At no time will a teacher be more important than now, in this new system. However, we will have to reshape the role and the classroom actions of the teacher. If we continue to train our educators the way we've always trained them, we will continue to be frustrated.

Second, we cannot make the mistake of thinking that the answer is to just buy the computers and stick them in the school. The intelligent deployment of technology is desperately needed. Digital natives, the learners, know much about technology because they've grown up with it.

Yet it's the digital immigrants, the generations of educators trained in a teaching system, making the deployment decisions. So we purchase expensive equipment, hardware and software, and believe that placing it on our campuses makes us innovative. Often a close look at how the equipment is used proves that the technology is being used simply to perform the same teaching tasks that support the teaching system. We have to be more intelligent and brave.

We have elements in our adopted system of education that teach children and adolescents to develop belief systems that trap them in a lifetime of learned helplessness. If we create mastery systems designed to ensure that every student masters what they should know, and we design the entire learning system around progress in a personalized environment that allows teachers to actually individualize their encouragement, their shepherding, on each child, future generations will recognize us as the educators who equipped our nation to step into, and benefit from, every resource at our disposal.

When discussions are had related to things like learned helplessness and students, it invariably turns to an acknowledgment of these things but an agreement that these things then have validity for certain groups of learners, the alternative kids, the ones who just "don't get it." That's what robs all students from the benefits of a mastery-based learning system. So let's get some clarity.

WHAT IS AN ENCURRICULAR LEARNING SYSTEM?

All learners must be involved in mastery-based learning. This has to be a given. All students, no matter their background, strengths, or needs, have to be in student-centered, self-directed education. These student-centered, self-directed environments should be called *encurricular learning systems*, "within the curriculum." The learner has the capacity to be within the curriculum, a vital and significant participant within the process, empowered to self-direct.

All learning opportunities in this country should be personalized and self-directed. These are two separate concepts, but they can interconnect in the classroom. The student-centered classroom should be both: personalized as it applies to a student being able to receive an accurate diagnosis of their learning and a route for increased learning that allows them to progress and add to their capacity to know more.

This is personal and can be done through digital technology platforms. Self-directed as it applies to adults handing off the decision-making element of the daily plan for learning to the student, closely monitoring that route consistently, and connecting with the learner through feedback and dialogue characterized by authentic engagement and motivation.

These two elements are nonnegotiable for the twenty-first century. *Encurricular learning systems are personalized and self-directed.* An encurricular learning system does not replace, minimize, or eliminate the teacher. *It repositions the teacher in the classroom.* It provides a more intelligent strategy for the teacher. It utilizes the best that the teacher can provide.

The encurricular learning system puts the student in a position to be taught responsibilities important for learning. It keeps the student motivated. It keeps the teacher engaged with kids rather than curriculum.

The traditional factory model of the last century was a teaching system focused on providing the best environment for teaching and teachers. *The encurricular model is a learning system* focused on the learner and learning.

An encurricular system ensures that every piece of content is covered, not just the pieces we have time to address within the time allotted during the day or year. The system ensures that every piece of the content is mastered. Progress is not measured through subjective grading.

Students must show mastery through objective measurements determined through technology. The teacher oversees the process individually for each student. Students make the decisions for the plan of learning each day. The teacher is able to engage with the student to guide and assist in the navigation of the learning path.

Learned helplessness isn't a characteristic of any one type of learner. We see disengaged students sitting in classrooms and walking the hallways every day. Encurricular learning systems engage the teacher with the learner and engage the learner with the curriculum. This process of learning maintains the high level of motivation for the student. It leverages the best of emerging technology and engaged educators. That's proving to be the key to solving the equations we have before us.

So we have the institutionalized teaching system that still functions as the foundation for our practice. It's all about how we teach. When we started the push for reform in our educational system, we began tinkering with the elements, but we were not going to shake the foundation too much because we mistakenly believed that this practice was the methodology assurance, our guarantee that, no matter what tinkering might occur, we could fall back on the fact that this practice guaranteed some form of learning. This teaching system is our industry standard.

However, just as the digital age has now transformed all we know and created new paradigms for those born into it, we should change that industry standard. Learning systems, encurricular learning systems that bring learners into an engaged participant status, are possible. Changing that industry standard, not just shaking up that foundation but replacing that foundation, should happen. Start there.

SUMMARY THOUGHTS

- There is a distinct difference between teaching systems, which focus on whether teaching is occurring, and learning systems, which focus on whether students are learning.
- Mastery-based learning, measuring progress, is the most objective process for grading in the classroom.
- Technology does not replace teachers, nor does it relegate teachers to a facilitator role, but transforms what the teacher will be doing in the classroom.
- Encurricular learning systems are defined by mastery-based, self-directed, and empowered learning opportunity in the classroom.

NOTES

1. M. E. P. Seligman, *Helplessness: On Depression, Development, and Death* (San Francisco: W. H. Freeman, 1975).

2. Howard Pitler and Elizabeth R. Hubbell, *Using Technology with Classroom Instruction that Works* (Denver, CO: ASCD, 2012).

Chapter 3

THE ARCHITECTURE OF A MASTERY-BASED SYSTEM

DOC'S STORY: "THE LIFE OF THE PARTY"

I loved her. By the time I knew her, she was well on in years and the sweetest person I had yet to meet, though at the age of seven, I had yet to meet too many people. But she was always sweet to me. And she always had a smile. She lived three houses down from us on our dirt road, where six houses sat along a couple-mile stretch.

That dirt road served as a street, a driveway, and a community link for all six families back in the 1960s. And it served as the runway for our adventures, the navigational map for our trek home at the end of the day, and the assurance that no money should be wasted on washing any car sitting in front of those six homes, as dust was just a part of life.

Those of us living on that road had a lot in common. Though it was the 1960s and though we lived in the country, we were way ahead when it came to modern technology. Because we had a "party line."

What's a party line? Simple. All six homes had telephones. Huge, black, clunky telephones. Loud appliances that took up a lot of room on the table or required industrial-sized screws to secure them to the wall. All six homes had one and all six had their own phone number. Today, our old one sits as a treasured relic from the past in my den.

On a party line, the phone lines were all connected. When you were on the phone, anyone in any of those six homes could listen to your phone conversation. And, even more comforting, when your phone rang, every phone in every house on that dirt road would ring. It's a party.

So when someone called, you and all your neighbors would answer. There would then be a lot of hellos and "who is this" and "who are you calling" going on for a minute or two. Working cooperatively, we could finally determine who the call was for and the five remaining neighbors would hang up and let you get on with your conversation. It was just a silent contract we had with each other. Everybody hangs up.

She felt it was her duty to know any important things going on in the lives of her neighbors. She was not nosy or intrusive. She just appointed herself that accountability and responsibility.

Did she ever think it was wrong to just pretend to hang up while silently staying on the line? Not sure. But I could hear her breathing. I loved her.

How should a mastery-based learning system look? What are the pieces that should drive the process? If we want to take twenty-first-century learning from isolated pockets of innovation and move it into a systemic, broad transformation, what are the most important elements that have to be evident and active in that system? What will be our paradigm? What should be our industry standard that is sustainable and defines education for the next 150 years?

First, it's important to make a clear distinction in what we refer to as mastery learning. As we discuss elsewhere in this book, there are some terms, definitions, and ideas that we have to understand in the twenty-first century. In doing so, we also have to know that these were hijacked, articulated, and made to fit within an adopted twentieth-century definition of teaching.

THE DISCONNECT THAT DELAYS

When ideas had great hope, especially when supported through research, these would typically receive enthusiastic and acceptable levels of acknowledgment, until the realization that these ideas had the potential to actually disrupt the classroom management system of teaching.[1]

Though never organized, it seemed there was a unified effort to give the appearance of adoption of these ideas while simultaneously molding, defining, and forcing the idea into the nonnegotiable system of teaching. The *appearance of acceptance*, only creating an interruption, rather than a disruption, of education.

We would have an idea presented to us that had great promise. No one could deny that the idea was beneficial for learners. And the idea had proven, or verifiable, results that further moved the idea to the front of the room. No one would dare refute the idea as it wouldn't be smart to do so and still state that the refuting party cared about learners. So the idea would start the process of moving up the line.

As more educators got involved, there was agreement that this idea might need to be implemented. Along with that realization came a growing fear, though, that adopting this idea in a systemic manner was going to actually mean that teachers would have to throw out some important elements of their training and experience. The classroom would have to change. The lesson plans might lose their significance. The administrative busyness of teaching would be radically different.

So the practitioners started tinkering. Official definitions to control, assign, and institutionalize the idea were formed and articulated. There was unspoken agreement among the authors of these definitions and those in the field. "We like this. We agree with this. This is good. And we want to do this. So knowing that how we teach is how learners learn, how can we take this and fit it in the system that we all agree cannot change? How can we make this work? Please, people, pull up a chair to the table of collaboration and let's put our heads together on this. We value everybody's thoughts on this and we have to reach a consensus on how we can make this work. First, let's decide who can best be helped by this new idea. Then we can make the Power Points, develop the training, and organize the roll-out."

Those definitions gave the appearance of acceptance while never actually gaining traction with the large populations of learners. The new idea was marginalized and moved to a corner, where it allowed everyone to say "yes" to it but never forcing anything to actually change. The disconnect between research and practice was created in the twentieth century where the protected teaching system was safe from disruption.

Researchers would confidently present those things they were discovering about learning. At the conference, all educators sitting in the rows of the session would nod their heads in agreement that this was good and right. Change was needed. And there was a sincere taking of notes in the crowd. Every document of the formal session notes were taken from the table at the back of the room and shoved into the briefcase, purse, or conference bag on the way out the door. There was a well-meaning intent to think about this and maybe even try some of it back at the campus.

Then Monday comes and they file into the room. Take attendance. Start the day. The teaching begins. Later, in the mid-week staff meeting, someone actually refers back to the idea from the conference. And the tinkering starts. It becomes a general ascent of "here's why it won't work here." There was an appreciation for the work and the research. There was an agreement that something should be done. But not here. Not in our classrooms and not on our campus.

"Maybe the district will organize something for all of us that we can experiment with and try this on for size just to see if it works. Maybe they won't, which will only confirm that our thoughts are correct in this. They just don't know our kids. They don't know our situation. And, by the way, do we even know if any of those speakers ever even taught in an actual classroom?" So research informed but never systemically disrupted the practice. Worse still, if the idea was so unavoidably true and good, the defined control isolating the idea would actually cause a false perception that the idea was actually changing practice. So an example is in order.

MASTERY LEARNING

Let's return to the concept of "mastery learning." This is a significant and important concept for education. Periodically, doctoral students are asked to define mastery of content, mastery learning. These students have been through every certification track and taken years of education courses. They are experienced and highly functional educators with proven records. When they see that question, that request to define mastery learning, they invariably create a well-articulated answer.

However, almost every educator confines that answer within the realm of special education. It's defined as a concept reserved for that specific area of education for kids who receive special education services. It's rarely defined as a general education concern.

When we discuss mastery learning as a general education issue, the debate begins. It's almost as if we are relegating the concept to a lesser degree as if we are diminishing the idea or somehow lowering the expectations for all students. First, that's offensive to the whole paradigm of special education. There can be a silent yet active acknowledgment that the expectations for special education students can afford to be lowered. That's not fair. And while there are countless numbers of special education teachers who maintain high levels of expectations for their students, there are some who just don't think their students can, or should, have the highest expectations.

However, that's not the point for this discussion. The point is that the idea of mastery learning is not a special education issue. It's a learning issue for all learners. So how did it get to be a definition and an idea that was officially part of only a segment of learning populations? When mastery of content was introduced in the twentieth century, it was not proposed as simply a special education matter. It started as an idea for personalized learning.

Personalized learning, individual and independent learning plans, were not just for certain students. Personalizing an education for learners was something that should be done not just for some students. It should happen for all. This concept didn't just suddenly appear out of thin air. We've known for years that we should be doing this.

However, the practice of mastery learning is robbed of its credibility because the practitioners, faced with the horrible truth that a wholesale adoption of this might cause too much classroom change, move it to a corner where it would appear that everyone agrees it is important, but the sweeping changes it could create should be reserved for a smaller population of learners. And the wheels keep turning in the teaching system.

Mastery learning, when mentioned now, gets lost in the silent agreement that it lessens rigor and lowers the expectation. Again, not fair even as applied to special education students and certainly not fair as ignored for general education students. It's been cornered and institutionalized so much that even the mention of the term conjures up a lesser form of teaching and learning.

And that's only one term, one beneficial idea that had potential when introduced, received agreement, but was then controlled by the way it was officially defined and designed in the field. That has happened repeatedly in education, so much so that hopeful ideas and research continues, but the disconnect between the research and the practice has itself become an acceptable practice in the industry of teaching.

We have a teaching system that has learned to move sideways. It doesn't move backward or forward. It continues to move sideways, acknowledging that desperate change is needed, that we have to do more and better for our kids. But we cannot change the teaching system in a way that changes the teaching. We still train the same way. We can actually teach our teachers how to continue doing the same things while knowing that they might be increasingly ineffective. But let's do the numbers and get the percentages. Shrug the shoulders because, really, what can you do? Do the best you can.

And all that will work. Until it won't. Why won't it work in our immediate future? Because the population of learners have grown up in a radically different world, so shrugging the shoulders will soon have to stop.

What we should be doing is using the concept of architecture in education. We have to become designers. In a world where delivery of content and information is readily available, we have to focus on making it accessible. Once we know it's accessible, we have to move from being *willing* to leverage that accessibility to being *prepared* and *ready* to leverage that accessibility.

THE RIGHT FOCUS

We have to move from being focused on the teacher and teaching to being focused on the learner and learning. If you ask the good teacher, the good teacher agrees. While there may be some who can't make it, the good teacher will actually be able to see the advantage and benefit of this shift in paradigms. And, using the resources available, administrators can design the campus and teachers can design the classroom to make sure learning happens for every learner.

So let's discuss some important elements of the architecture for a mastery-based system of learning. One of the most important elements that has to be addressed is measurement. Subjective grading, though important for some areas, has to become a minimized practice for a mastery-based practice. What should be measured is the progress of the student.

If we can design a learning system that ensures students can only progress if they master the content and information, the idea of subjective grading isn't as important as whether the student is progressing effectively. We should create the system in a way that guarantees a student cannot move forward unless, or until, the knowledge that should be gained from the content has been learned in an effective way. At that point, the monitoring of the student, the watchful eye of the parent and educator, should be on the progress of the learner.

How easy is it in a subjective environment to always blame the teacher when things go wrong for us? How little value is sometimes placed on classroom testing when we know we will have chances to negotiate, charm, or bargain our way through even if we don't do well? Conversely, how many external variables factor in the high-stakes testing of a teacher when the teacher is in charge of the subjective assessment and grading?

Think about it. The teacher is supposed to be fair. But is that always true, in every case? Is there no room to admit that the teacher can, and does, make mistakes? Or worse, can be unfair. All while escaping accusations of being unfair by being offended at the mere suggestion that it could happen. And what about those accusations? How many good teachers have been accused by a parent or a student? Knowing that a certain grade will cause drama, how many times does the teacher not do it simply because it's not worth it?

We all imagine in our mind that teacher who's getting a little non-confessed thrill and silent satisfaction when the red marks occur on some students' assignments. We all know that teacher who just enjoyed it. But again, think about it. Is that really fair? To accuse a teacher of purposely punishing some students through grading seems a little harsh. Any teacher reading the last few sentences might have been a little offended.

But any teacher reading the last few sentences could probably name at least one teacher they feel could be accurately accused of committing these very offenses, maybe a colleague or a childhood teacher from their own past or that college professor. That's the problem. Leaving the grading and assessment in the hands of the teacher cannot happen in a mastery system because it has to be objective. And being pure and objective is not possible for a human.

Assessment and grading should become parts of a technology-based practice. Digital platforms can diagnose the targeted areas of deficiency in the learner. Additionally, these same platforms have the ability to prescribe the route for the learner in a personalized way.

We don't want to totally remove a teacher from the process, though. But we need to use their intelligence much more strategically. We take intelligent individuals and force them into a system that doesn't allow them to spread that intelligence around. We demand that they do a uniform grading practice that depletes their energy and decreases the chances that it can be done equally and fairly for every learner.

This is not an indictment on teachers. It's an indictment on the system. We mistakenly believe that a human can approach every learner equally, engage with every grading situation equally, and complete the task of grading equally. Any cursory knowledge about the human condition and how we consciously and subconsciously operate tells us that this is improbable at best and impossible at worst. It can't be done.

If we argue that taking the human out of the process is dehumanizing, the argument is only strengthened that grading should be objective and absent of human trappings. No one wants their ability to progress in life based solely on one person because we know how fallible people can be. If one has to depend on success solely based on the ability to charm, we lose every time. True academic measurement demands that it be done absent the perceptions of the assessment process. This can best be done by technology.

So what would we ask teachers to assess? What would we ask of them in elements of assessment? Simply put, mastering content and information is not enough. It's vital to the learning process. But it's not going to ensure everything we should want from our education system. Students should prove their learning. This, on the face of it, could be done with an objective mastery exam.

The mastery exam should be high stakes. But that exam has to be attempted when readiness is proven. And that's where the teacher has to be engaged with the learner. Just as high-level doctoral candidates have to show their learning before being allowed to move forward in their construction and studies in a doctorate, students should be required to give an "oral defense" of their understanding and knowledge to earn the right to take that mastery exam.

In the end, the student will be attempting an exam with high stakes, one that determines whether they can move forward in their learning journey. So they should be able to prove they've earned the right to take that exam. That brings higher value to the exam. That makes the student work for the right thing. The student should earn the right and the teacher should have a relationship with the student that can accurately assess whether the student is ready for that high-stakes test.

In the model that will be described later, teachers are the most important element of the system. But you won't find a teacher preparing one lesson plan, making any lesson preparations, or controlling the decision making of the exact content or subjects a student engages with each day. The system is compared to the modern digital GPS system that everyone seems to have in their cars or their hands in the twenty-first century. And the teacher is the satellite.

More description and greater detail about this concept will be provided later, but suffice it to say that if there's no satellite connected to the GPS in your car, you have a cool computer map, a car, and a driver, but the system breaks down. You need that satellite. And we need the teacher. Think about these things later in the book, but for the purposes of this chapter, know that the teacher is crucial.

CLASSICAL EDUCATION

Not only are teachers and mastery learning important to the architectural design of an encurricular learning system, but elements of classical and character education also have to be present in a twenty-first-century model as well. However, it's important to understand how this is defined because a fundamental misunderstanding of this statement can create a fundamental flaw in our thinking about twenty-first-century learning systems if we're not careful. So let's briefly define how this is articulated.

In education, we have content: what is taught and learned (hopefully). There is also concept: how we think about the teaching and learning. And there is practice: how we do what we do. While we have to radically change our concept (how we do what we do) and that requires an understanding of the concept (what we think about what we are doing), we should strengthen the content (what is actually learned). Students in the twenty-first century have to leave us with a higher level of understanding about the world they live in as an adult and how to navigate that world.

Classical education content has always been the foundation we should strive for when we teach current and future generations. Some things don't change and classical content, what kids should know, has to be protected. The studies connected to ancient civilizations, Latin and other languages, classical literature, the Trivium, have been at the heart of education for centuries, and just because it's now the twenty-first century doesn't change that.

Some think that classical education only defines a methodology, the "way we teach." The thought is that "classical" only means structured, disciplined, rigid teacher-driven methods with a rap on the knuckles for any student not paying attention. "Sit straight and pay attention, son. I'm talking." Nothing could be further from the truth.

Classical education is, first and foremost, content: rich in historical, proven, and time-honored knowledge that teaches truth, beauty, goodness, character, and wisdom. We should be changing our methods, but we have to protect the content. A student in the twenty-first century still needs a classical education and that won't change just because tools and resources progress and innovate our process. What kids should know is timeless and should remain in place to ensure the passing of classical education to next generations.

We often toss out terms such as *rigor*, *critical thinking*, and *higher-order thinking*. Most, though using those terms, don't know what they mean, don't know how to define them, and use them as buzzwords. We get caught in this high-sounding cycle that throws these terms around while diminishing the importance of facts and knowledge. We have to understand that there is a body of knowledge that a student should know when they leave us with a diploma. Yes, teaching them how to think is vital, but not at the expense of teaching them what they should know as well.

Our educational system, how we structure, think about, and design our schools, needs transformation. That does not mean changing the classical content needed for now and in the future. It means the methodology, the teaching process, the tools, and the resources must be changed, deployed, and utilized in a disruptive manner that completely transforms the industrial assembly line school.

A liberal arts, classical content curriculum has to maintain a place of prominence in our classrooms. We often replace it with an emphasis on self-esteem. We tell kids whatever they think is okay, that they are just great, and we pat them on the head from an early age. We emphasize the "self" as being most important. Then once we've convinced them they are the center of the universe, we ask them to make value judgments and choose their path. As adolescents, they grow confused because the world doesn't continue to pat them on the head and they can't understand why their behavior is challenged.

Character education does not place "self" at the center. Sometimes character education is hard or tough to take. It doesn't tell me I'm always right. Sometimes I'm wrong. It teaches me self-reflection rather than self-esteem. It teaches me that I have a debt to those around me. It doesn't pat me on the head. The content of a classical education focuses on those things that are most important for us, the body of knowledge required to be a successful adult, and those character traits necessary to appreciate and understand how we can thrive in a twenty-first-century world.

Self-esteem is vital and teachers can motivate and engage in ways that strengthen the elements of self-esteem. Value judgment is important for anyone, but if we are valuing and choosing in this life, we are most successful if we have been exposed to learning opportunities that develop character within us.

We should be teaching our students to be systems thinkers. We should be teaching them how to not only access and receive information, but also how to analyze and think about that information. Sadly, most teachers believe this is only possible if they control the process, lecturing their way through the content. That's practice and methodology. If we believe that our planning, preparing, and presenting the content each day is the structure of a classical education, we missed the mark once again. We've missed the opportunity to connect and engage again.

In a mastery-based learning system, students can actually work together. After all, isn't that how the world works? We work together and we learn from each other. In an encurricular learning system, this is possible because learning is a process in which we should be leveraging every available resource and opportunity.

Students in the encurricular learning world can work together and increase their knowledge with a blending of technology, teachers, and each other. As they learn and progress, it's understood that each student has to prove mastery objectively, but getting to that point can be a collaborative process if that's how specific students learn best.

The architecture of the twenty-first-century, student-centered, mastery-based encurricular learning system is possible for all learners and the isolated pockets of this are produced in efforts in numerous regions even now. There are examples of these elements already being done.[2] However, to transform rather than reform education, we have to stop thinking this should just be experimental and alternative.

CHANGING THE RIGHT THING

The greatest strategy to really change education is to change educators. What we do and how we do it for the twenty-first-century student is our highest challenge. The most significant educators are learners who don't know everything, but will take the risks necessary for the sake of those they shepherd daily.

We're losing a lot these days. In the standards-driven climate that doesn't know how to measure learning, we're pushing more and more passion out of educators, kids, and parents. We're losing opportunity, kids, and time. By fiercely holding on to the traditional teaching systems from the last century, we're increasing the populations of disengaged students across the nation. We're wasting the brilliance of classroom teachers, the intelligence of risk takers, and time.

We should not be "building a house" in our districts that stands as our monument to innovation. We should be "building a city" that transforms our entire way of thinking when we think about education. And the architecture of that city uses the building materials of student empowerment, technology delivery, and assessment of classical content, engaged educators for each learner the right way and progress through mastery as our only measurement.

We can change this if we use the available resources provided through a digital delivery system, stop the practice of defining teaching as merely sharing information, and start teaching the greater elements of wisdom and character, designing twenty-first-century classrooms that blend the best of technology with the best of teaching, empowering students with decision making and giving them the ability to learn in an environment that connects the educator with the student, every student. And we have to do it systemically, across the board. As we will see in the model later in this book, we have opportunities to do it now.

SUMMARY THOUGHTS

- Mastery-based learning should have the high standard of 90 percent for students to be allowed to progress to the next level.
- Technology eliminates subjective grading from the classroom.
- Teachers can focus on assessing students' readiness to take mastery exams in the encurricular learning system.
- Even as we make transformative changes in our education system, we must remain committed to the established and reliable classical education content.

NOTES

1. C. Christensen, C. W. Johnson, and M. B. Horn, *Disrupting Class: How Disruptive Innovation Will Change the Way the World Learns* (New York: McGraw-Hill, 2008).

2. M. B. Horn and H. Staker, *Blended: Using Disruptive Innovation to Improve Schools* (San Francisco, CA: Jossey-Bass, 2014).

Chapter 4

THE FOUR DETERMINANTS OF AN ENCURRICULAR LEARNING SYSTEM

DOC'S STORY: "SOMETHING IS TERRIBLY PONG IN MY WORLD"

I remember the moment when the wheels came off my wonderful prehistoric life and were replaced by floating ghosts being chased by gobbling gremlins, space invaders invading my space, and effortless upgrading/updating became just one more thing I couldn't do without tons of frustration and fear.

The gritty details: The local pizza place in a small Texas town where everybody gathered after church. Me, a teenager who, at least in the mid-1970s, was relatively cool and in control. We always came here and we always knew what we were going to order and we always knew how our evening would proceed. Good pizza, good friends, and a great place to hang out. Little did I know that my world of revered analog dreams was about to disappear into a black hole.

As I entered, I saw something I'd never seen before. Over by the far wall was a large object, sort of like a large table shaped like a huge box about three feet in height. Seated at either end were two teenage guys staring intently down at the box. I walked over just to see what was going on. A small crowd of kids my age was assembled and staring at the box as well.

And that's when I saw it. A large white dot was moving back and forth across a glass screen on top of the box. Each boy had a large dial on his end he was turning and as he turned the dial, a small white "line" on his end of the box would move left and right in front of the particular guy turning his dial. And if the line was placed into the path of the dot, and if the dot touched that line, it would immediately change direction and reverse itself on the screen, flowing back the other way. It appeared the objective of the game was to make sure that dot hit your line, sending the dot the other way. If you missed, the other guy got a point.

What just happened? How is that possible? It's a picture of a dot? Hitting a picture of a line? But acting like a real tennis ball. I stood transfixed, suddenly realizing my world had changed. And since that fateful Texas night, the digital immigrant (which I didn't even know at the time would be my official title in thirty years) watched as his homeland, his native country, slowly changed from a kingdom he once ruled to a strange world of mobile devices with endless information accessible with a tap and swipe.

The most recent period in our history saw confusion become a natural, accepted thought of all of us toward our educational system. Were we competitive? Was the schooling of our children even effective in preparing them to take their place in society as citizens? And what about the increasing numbers of dropouts? Should we be testing children or testing teachers? Does any of this even matter?

These questions, and many more, have us constantly looking for answers, trying to find the keys to the car that will drive us to the right destination. We can't find those keys, though we look everywhere and we try to retrace our steps. We try to remember where we last saw those keys. We pick things up, put them down, look behind things, and check every nook and cranny trying to locate those elusive keys.

Not the strongest analogy, but an analogy still. We search everywhere for the keys that get us to where we want to go with our students. So as is typical, we ride the three-year cycle of "change" in our districts and charters. We buy it, train it, put it in our classrooms, measure it, and let it run its course until the new one gets here. Then it starts all over again. It's a pretty good system for the continual, never-ending life of a school.

In fact, it keeps us busy, with our new urgencies and calls for immediate improvements. But it's cyclical and we know it. It's just a part of the system. It's a revolving door syndrome that tries to project itself as an evolving door syndrome. But we never actually evolve to anything transformed.

However, we have entered an interesting time of life. This world has changed dramatically in this new century. The current generations of educators were children in school during the waning years of the last century and it was a very progressive time related to innovations and new ideas.

Each of these innovations was cool and created incremental changes in life itself. The push-through tab to open a can of soda, video cassettes, something called a Walkman, and even Post It notes all came on the proverbial "scene" in the seventies. While these things were always cool, they were not necessarily life changing.

Now we are well into the new century and we've watched this grow from a simple game of Pong, which our children have never played, to a world of communication and information that has connected and disconnected so many things in so many ways. While every industry that hopes to thrive, not just survive, this new world has aggressively accepted and adopted the new language and the new opportunities, education by and large has yet to make systemic changes that not only leverage these new technologies, but also become the leader of industry that shows the way for all of us.

Sadly, we've used an emotional argument, the human factor, as our reason for dragging our feet. By using that argument, we are unwisely painting ourselves into a corner where we will be forced to leave the room one day because when the time comes that our ranks are only filled with digital natives, they will set us aside due to irrelevance. We will become the *irrelevant elephant* in the room, if you will.

EDUCATION REFORM

However, an interesting thing has happened to education reform. From its birth in the last quarter of our recent century, education reform began as a reaction to the calls for change brought about by the major studies and research conducted, including *A Nation at Risk*, that identified our education system as lacking the ability to keep us competitive on a world stage.[1] So in order to ensure our children were able to stay afloat in the world, and remember this was before digital had even come on the scene, there began a unified, concerted, and national effort to improve our schools.

It is clearly, without apology, an effort to improve the system, to reform the system. It was not meant to transform the system. There were certainly no thoughts about abandoning the adopted way of life and practice within the American classroom. We just needed to tweak the system, reshape the lesson planning, and collaborate a little more.

Test the kids more, train the teachers more. In other words, reform. Take the form of it, push here, pull there, until the system we knew as our way of life was perfected. That model of education reform took hold and was established on a national scale and we closed out the last century with an environment where we had our education system, the vehicle we used to school our kids, and our education reform system, the "shop" where we were continually trying to fix, repair, or upgrade the vehicle.

Enter the twenty-first century. Just before the clocks rolled over to bring in the year 2000, technology was forging new roads for us. We tentatively got "online" and even began "chatting" to each other and sending documents through "email." While this certainly had been going on for a while in business and other areas, it started reaching the national consumer in the late 1990s and it was fun and new. We still weren't quite sure about all of it. But it was something we could add to our list of available ways to communicate: the phone, the post office, and now the computer. Technology was here and we were glad of it.

Then digital came along. It became much easier not only to use the new technology, but it also became affordable. Fast forward to today and we can now say that it's become necessary for us. In our ordinary lives, doing our ordinary things in our ordinary ways, digital technology has become a way of life.

Most industries saw it and began aggressively searching for ways to use it. When digital changed everything, these same industries even transformed their adopted systems of creating their products. They started learning the new language and rethinking all they had previously known in order to meet the needs of their customers who were assimilating these new ways in their ordinary world.

And the vehicle of our education system kept moving forward. And education reform kept working on it, tweaking it, and reshaping it. But there was no national effort that understood that we needed a *systemic transformation*. Nationally, we began an even stronger effort to just test the kids and test the teachers using the old system.

Standards and accountability policies and practice overcame the entire environment of education and became the latest tweaking or reshaping of the vehicle. And what has it done? Only made us more convinced that we are not doing a great job.

THE ENDLESS CYCLE

We measure schools, we measure teachers, and we always do it by testing kids. It doesn't matter whether the child had a peaceful night of study the night before the test or spent the night lying awake because they were afraid and worried about things that only adults should worry about. Every learner is different and unique, each characterized by so many variables, but that doesn't seem to matter in a standards-driven testing environment.

So the cycle continues. Test the kids in the manner that seems logical, defined by the adopted method of schooling. Set the percentage of failures we will accept as our measure of success. Often the number doesn't even have to be set until after the tests are graded and results are known.

Once that occurs, declare the school good or bad based on the fact that this school failed a lower or higher number of students compared with other schools in the region, state, or nation. Once those announcements are made, we can tell the parents, the paper, and everybody else how less or more terrible the school is according to our intellectual system of measuring education.

That's when the education reform cycle kicks in. Send in the consultants and buy the state assessment preparation curriculum designed specifically for the test. This is not the "what every learner should know to grow as a person" material. This is the "what every tester should know to pass the test" material.

Get out the teacher rubrics, all based on the ability to achieve the lowest number of failures. Identify the teachers who did the worst. Never fire them, but certainly never truly analyze why the results were not as good as the teacher across the hall, as that takes too much work actually analyzing every learner.

Scare the teacher, stress the campus, and panic the parent. And if the kid didn't do well, it's because the teacher is bad, the school is bad, and the district is bad. But wait. If the percentage of failures is low enough, then it changes. The teacher is good but this kid is bad. The school is great but this kid is bad. In our adopted method of schooling based on a standards-driven process, we do not have to engage or motivate. We just need to test. The goal is that we have to shoot for the lowest number of failures possible so that we can deflect the failure to the kid, not the system. It's a game. Though so many are saying that the old way is gone, it isn't.

ARE WE CREATIVE?

However, in the digital world, there has risen an increasing demand for something new, something that recognizes the fact that these learners are growing up in a different world, shaped by digital technology. So we all know we need change. But this change demands creation, not innovation. To improve a system that the kid three generations from now won't accept or function in isn't good enough. To just make it better or modified won't cut it.

It's become increasingly obvious that everybody wants to be seen as creative and cool. It can almost reach a carnival atmosphere pitch with sideshows and awesome circus tents. We understand it's "new." We understand it's "tech." We hear *personalized*, *individualized*, *project*, *digital*, and all other twenty-first-century terms being thrown out there, printed in bold, and placed on buildings as if we just created a new language.

Honestly, some very creative and credible educators have been using those terms and doing those things for years. They were doing it when it wasn't cool.

Suddenly everybody's doing it and taking credit. That's okay, except for one thing. They didn't build that train, they're just a passenger. But the headlines of a newly discovered way of teaching kids aren't new or discovered. It's just buying the ticket and finding the seat on the train.

The fear is that the things we will begin to accept as new and innovative won't address the things we need to change. Changing names, buying computers, and kids sitting in a circle are not going to change anything. *The real fear and the real danger is that we can actually fashion a culture of reform without ever really changing anything.*

There's just a lot of the traditional system that adults may not be willing to give away. By doing so, we would have to throw out so much of our training, so much of our beliefs, and so much of our comfort. Instead, we opt on *looking* like we are different, new, or reformed.

It's almost as if, knowing that our public demands reform, many schools, districts, campuses, and administrators do nothing more than just put on a new and different piece of jewelry to prove "they're still pretty" in this century. Sometimes that can even mean simply changing the name of something to sound new and classy.

We're trying to please our public. Throw the hardware in, change the name to tech-something, and you've got a better-looking date to the prom. But if you look beneath the makeup, it's still the same. Are we creative?

Let's make a distinction. There's innovation and there's creation. We see a lot of innovation. We are confined in traditional systems by the consuming idea of time and location. We hear about innovation, but we don't hear about systems that discard these ideas. So it ends up at the same place, at the same time. Except we now find we're just coming up with ways to do the same traditional system with computers. Jewelry.

The reason we have to stop being innovative and start being creative has nothing to do with how much technology we put in our schools. The reason we have to stop being innovative and start being creative has nothing to do with how much technology we have in our classrooms. The reason we have to start being creative is because of the new paradigm and the consuming technology they already have and already use, and how that digital has changed them. They? The students. The digital native is different from anything we've encountered before.

Let's face it. They are not impressed, awed, or moved by the ever-increasing upgrade every month. They just expect it and use it as it arrives. They don't consider any new app or program to be a life-changing event. They yawn as they tap and swipe their screens.

It's not the emergence of so much technology that creates the demand for systemic change. These are simple tools and we've always had bigger, better, and brighter tools introduced consistently, continually, and constantly from day one to now. The advancement of the tool doesn't necessarily demand an entire transformation of a highly structured schooling system.

We can adequately and effectively place these tools in our established culture of education and use them to make teaching better. And if we want to limp along, that's good enough.

But the wheels come off when we fix our eyes on these twenty-first-century tools, believe that these tools are the definition of twenty-first-century progress, and focus on decorating our schools with a centerpiece arrangement of these tools to somehow qualify us as a twenty-first-century model of academic excellence.

Conversely, detractors don't like the tools. So they cast their lines way too far in their arguments. And just like those who focus on the jewelry just to look pretty, opponents focus on the tools to instill fear in those considering change: replacing teachers, minimizing the importance of teachers, and dehumanizing the classroom. This all just focuses on the tool.

It seems that we glorify, idolize, or vilify the tool. So the debate continues and time marches on. Somewhere in the background, they're still tapping, swiping, and yawning. Again, it's not the emergence of technology. It's not the tool that demands, forces, and requires a truly creative national transformation of the entire schooling system. It's the kid.

Digital natives are different from any previous generation of learners. They have a different approach. They start and end at different points than learners in the past. Kids are kids. That doesn't change. But these generations truly are different.

The car changed American life. The phone changed American life. Throughout our history, there have been true creations that dramatically changed the way we do life. But nothing in recent history has made such a dramatic and powerful difference in everything we do as the emergence of technology in just a few short years. Watching it force change upon us has been a cool experience. But imagine those who were born into it and are growing up with it now as a routine part of life. These kids are different. They will, and do, think differently.

Somebody has to be creative now. We can't afford to wait until the outdated system implodes, whether it be a financial, theoretical, or practical implosion. We can't just prop it up and hope it works out. To be innovative is nice, but it will only survive the traditional three-to-five-year lifecycle until another Band-Aid has to be applied.

We have to address what we call the *four determinants of the encurricular learning systems*. These are nonnegotiable elements that define the major components of the traditional system of education that must be addressed if you are going to be responsive to today's student. We can genuinely measure or define anything calling itself transformative by these four elements. Any so-called innovation not meeting the requirements of the four determinants is merely reformation, only tweaking the industrial system that refuses to change.

These elements are not necessarily dependent on technology, though technology makes these elements accessible and available for educators to create rather than simply innovate learning opportunities for students.

Knowing how to walk onto a campus, carefully analyze the "new" way, and measure it against these determinants can help us assess 1) whether it's a true twenty-first-century creative transformative system or simply an innovative reforming that "props up" the old system and 2) whether it has the capacity to leverage the best of the teacher and the best of technology for today's learner. Should we not intentionally agree that these elements are important, we will continue to confuse the potential to see creative transformation for new learners.

THE FOUR DETERMINANTS

Time

If students cannot direct their process of learning related to time, it's not creative, innovative, different, or new. Students should be able to see their learning, set their goals daily, and move forward within a reasonable framework of supervision and monitoring.

Any element of a system that defines, confines, or controls the pace diminishes and dampens the creative essence of the system. Be as tech as you want to be, but putting technology in a confining timed system neutralizes any twenty-first-century potential. Our systems, from campus level to state levels across our nation, are timed, and the new system has to confront this component.

The most serious hindrance to true change in education is the time factor. We've built a system designed to run on time. While appreciating the efforts of some in education reform, there doesn't appear to be a lot of risk taking out here that addresses the fact that we time our students. There isn't a lot of curriculum being produced, published, and distributed that addresses the fact that we have a strict adherence to a calendar.

We don't leave a child "behind."[2] We lose that child. Even the word *behind* means that he or she couldn't keep up and he or she needs to catch up. Keep up and catch up with whom? You? Me? The majority of the class?

The fact that we have a strict date for a state test (and call it an end of course test) proves that it's all on a time schedule. One would think that "end of course" simply means when you, in your own time, complete the course. That may be today, tomorrow, or a month ago.

Freshman, sophomore, junior, senior. Ask any high school kid and they'll let you know, by using those time-based designations, how far along they are and how much farther they have to go before being handed their diploma.

We all admit that they don't learn the same way, but we still time them. We love to talk about learning styles, but we need to start considering learning time. We're so obsessed with an organized timed day, semester, and year that we'll even chunk in a lot of nonessential stuff that guarantees we keep to the schedule. The timed pacing of learning is often the most frustrating element of school.

There can be just as many disengaged students frustrated by the mind-numbing timed pace of a course as those frustrated because they just couldn't keep up with their peers. To continue in a timed system means we don't understand it isn't necessary or we are not sure what to do with kids unless we control as much of their waking hours as possible.

Location

Long ago, we had distance learning. Good or bad, it took courage and demands our respect. However, the element of location means much more than virtual or online learning, which are highly regarded and can be as rigorous as any classroom.

If a system is designed to only recognize or offer new content learning in one location (wherever the teacher is at the time), it isn't a creative twenty-first-century system. We shouldn't have to expound upon the current and emerging opportunities for learning that eliminates the need for location-specific requirements. However, the idea begs some examples.

Bad weather days become a nonsignificant issue if location is taken out of the equation. Ten feet of snow the night before? No problem because the students are able to access learning no matter where they may be. No more wringing of hands by superintendents afraid of losing so much state funding on those days when an exorbitant number of students are absent because of bad weather conditions.

Beneficial opportunities such as extended family trips become a nonsignificant issue if location is taken out of the equation. Honestly, times like this can sometimes be even more fruitful for a kid than sitting in a classroom. But we don't excuse them because there are rules and the kid needs to be in their seat when that bell rings. But if location isn't a hindrance to learning, the learner doesn't have to be tied to the combo desk.

Now before anyone shouts the obvious, someone will point out that we refer to these examples in a technology-based platform. So what about the student who doesn't have access to technology at home? What about the shutting down of local power sources during those storms? What if someone trips over the giant extension cord providing current to all that Internet?

And the answer is simple. We cannot mistake technology as being the answer. It seems that's become the faux determinant for twenty-first-century education. And it isn't. It's not technology that defines a new learning system. If we fall for that, it becomes too easy to look twenty-first century while making no changes for learner.

Creative learning systems will never be defined or confined by technology. The four determinant list does not include computers. Independent, self-directed, and personalized student-centered learning can be paper based as easily as technology based. Technology is not the make or break issue when it comes to location.

Summer vacations? Spring break? All of it is connected to a mindset of location. If you're not in the seat at the appointed time with the appointed teacher, learning can't happen. But in the twenty-first century, K–12 education should not be subject to location. If it is, it isn't creative. The brick and mortar is still valuable, but what we do inside that building may have to change and open up new frontiers for education.

Delivery

Once, while walking down a hallway of a middle school, a building administrator passed an open classroom door and as he passed by, he noticed a very quiet, orderly room full of tenth-grade students. No one was up participating in any tenth-grade shenanigans. In fact, no one was doing anything.

The students were quietly talking to each other, but there was a feeling that something just wasn't quite right. He stepped just inside the door and realized that the teacher was not present at the moment. He asked the students what they were doing. They responded they were in American history. He said he knew they were in American history class, but the question was *what were they doing*?

Again, American history. No, he replied, *what are you doing right now*? They then realized what he meant and explained that the teacher had gone to the office to take a quick phone call. They were waiting for her to return so they could begin class. No teacher, no learning. Sure, the teacher could have given them a quick exercise from the unit to work on until she returned. However, that's not the point.

Content is content. Information is information. That's not teaching. Delivering the content to learners can be accomplished in myriad ways, digital technology being the latest. Paper-based curriculum designed for today's learner can be delivered to students in very creative ways.

Peer and social learning networks, even beyond the walls of a classroom, can happen now. Good educators will know how to be creative in delivering content to students. And then there's the obvious. Technology, and specifically digital technology, has opened doors of opportunity for content to be delivered more than ever, better than ever. And the advantage of a technology-based delivery system almost demands that it be considered as the only option in today's environment.

If a student is being taught through direct lecture styles only from a designated teacher in the classroom, the design is not creative. No educator admits to lecture teacher-driven instruction any longer. However, there is need for some of this in the teaching learning equation. The problem is that we now have access to teachers, professors, tutors, and even digital instructors worldwide, yet we don't use them very often.

When a student needs to hear a lecture or be taught directly how to solve a problem or learn new material, that student has the capability of learning from someone better than you, me, or that teacher in the classroom. At its purest, the teacher in the classroom should be involved in the most minimal way in offering direct content instruction. However, the primary goal of that classroom adult should be to mentor kids and change lives, increasing student motivation and engagement so learners can learn.

Measurement

If a student is being given a traditional grade for new content learning, controlled by a subjective individual, and the student's progress is determined by that subjective grade, the design is not creative. No matter how frustrated or offended a person may become by this assertion, it doesn't change the fact that subjective grading cannot be perfect.

Assessment by subjective educators can be done, but it shouldn't be for content learning. Students should master content and the bar should be set high, 90 percent at a minimum. Technology can do this better than any teacher.

So much has already been stated about the element of grading. And we won't return to that. But related to the need to measure the latest reformation, an inspection of how students are measured and assessed is required.

PULLING OUT THE TAPE MEASURE ON THE FOUR DETERMINANTS

So in this day of so much education reform, we can vigorously debate the legitimacy of almost anything labeled new, as long as it has some form of computer utilization, or students collaborating, or teachers trying something different. It reaches the point that it's difficult to even argue that any of it isn't new or improved. But if all we're trying to do is improve the old system, then the list of options can fill pages of three-ring binders. And those binders can get heavy after a while.

So let's be clear. New and improved isn't a bad thing, as long as you're willing to admit that it's not twenty-first-century learning that you're creating. Rather, it's twenty-first-century teaching you're supporting and protecting. It's just a tweak here and there to make the old vehicle run better. To call it twenty-first century takes the innocent attempt to look better and feel better about what we are doing and layers in a disingenuous quality to it.

It can be analogous to a decision of whether to buy a new car or improve the car you already drive. You can research and learn how to install an interior dashboard kit. You can purchase the kit online and do it on a Saturday afternoon. You can have the local dealer install a spoiler and tint the windows. You can make that same car look even nicer. You can keep your old car, but it now has the accoutrements you wanted, the features that you wanted in a new car. But it's still your old car.

So if we are only going to talk about cars, you'd probably agree that doing that might be a good thing. But we're not talking about cars. Even though the windows are tinted and you like it, it's still the old car. Even though the "feeling" you have while driving it is nicer because of that wood grain interior, it's still the old car.

In education, that's all we're doing sometimes. We are not trading in the car. We are not getting the better car or the higher quality vehicle. We're just adding some features, tinkering with the windows, tires, and audio system.

We are buying the computers and getting the kids to circle up. But if you look, you still see the whole thing is dependent on specific location, time, measurement, delivery, or a combination of those four determinants. And any violation of any one of these determinants disqualifies it from being the new car. And we're not talking about cars. We're talking about kids.

We have to reshape our paradigm about learning and teaching. We have to transform rather than reform. But if we do, we have to first know how to measure any twenty-first-century educational attempts. Using the four determinants affords us a reliable way to decide if we are truly transforming and reshaping our paradigm or just tweaking the old one.

SUMMARY THOUGHTS

We can measure and assess whether a classroom environment is an encurricular system focused on learning by using the four determinants:

- *Time*: students are allowed to progress through their studies at an accelerated or slower pace determined by their personal strengths and needs.
- *Location*: focused learning and progress is not confined to the classroom.
- *Delivery*: content for learning is delivered to students in a variety of methods, the primary being technology.
- *Measurement*: all grades and learning assessments are done through technology.

NOTES

1. National Commission on Excellence in Education, *A Nation at Risk: The Imperative for Educational Reform* (Washington, D.C.: U.S. Government Printing Office, 1983).
2. No Child Left Behind, U.S. Department of Education-2001, Public Law of PL 107-110.

Chapter 5

THE NEW FLIGHT PLAN

DOC'S STORY: "WHAT'S A SELFIE?"

I loved the view. You could have your ringside seat, your hometown bleacher, and your press box. Nothing matched the angle I had for high school football games years ago. Long, long ago, I had the honor of filming the high school football games. I would record every play, then rush the film to a local drop-off point each Friday night after the game, where it would be picked up to be developed overnight.

The following morning, the coaches would pick it up at the location and view it with the team in the fieldhouse during Saturday practice. The coolest part of it all was the reserved spot I had during the game for filming.

This wonderful view was afforded me on what we called the "crow's nest." This was a very small platform that extended out from the metal light pole at the fifty-yard line, welded to the pole and perched precariously out over the playing field. Risky in the best of circumstances.

While serving as a great place to watch the game, this perch offered little room to perform the tasks required for filming. The camera of choice? An old wind-up that was most likely used by our forefathers to film the first Thanksgiving.

Insert a metal key in the camera, wind it until it's sufficiently primed, look through the lens, and focus on the line of scrimmage. Push the metal button to start filming when the ball is hiked, and hopefully follow the action while the camera whirs mechanically until the play is finished and you remove your index finger from the metal button.

You had to pay attention because a game would require about six rolls of film and changing out those rolls on that perch was acrobatic and stressful. Unscrew several screws from the metal casing, yank the roll out of the camera, pop that roll into the protected cardboard box, get the new roll, thread it through the camera, get it started properly, screw the casing back into place, insert the metal key, wind the camera, focus on the line of scrimmage and start it all over again.

All this between plays because the play you miss might be the play that would have secured our spot in the state playoffs.

Funny. Not once did the thought ever occur to me, "They should make an app for this."

In the new century, there is no doubt that the face of education will change. In fact it's rapidly changing already. But the change will soon become systemic. This change will not just be a modification or minor shift in how we do what we do. This change will not be an upgrade supported by tweaked professional development slightly different from last year's sessions. This change will be a major upheaval, a disruption that transcends the lesson planning, the bell systems, and the sectioned day neatly divided and coordinated into colored blocks on the poster boards and easels in the teacher's lounge.

Communication has transcended the old telephones that used to sit on our kitchen counters, cameras have become handheld devices that allow anyone with a wired connection to see what we just shot through the lens, and global paradigms have become a way of life. The significant part of this is that, while that life is largely a part of the big picture of a digital immigrant's life, that life IS the big picture of the digital native's life. In other words, though these things are new to us, they are all our students have known.

Though the coming change for education has largely been staved off by traditional systems having convinced us that our national accepted idea that learners will only learn if we teach them a certain way, the learners are getting older. While patience has been the order of the day when considering wholesale change in education, that sun is setting and we will see a transformation occur as soon as the ability to create a systemic transformation is realized and adopted. Why? Because it has to. No longer will the arguments that have held strong opposing these changes be valid because the listeners will know they don't hold water.

The number of students in our nation will not experience any appreciable decrease. The learner will benefit from the changes as our school systems become highly focused student-centered learning systems designed to ensure personal opportunities for every child and adolescent. Our workforce will benefit from graduates being better prepared to enter their doors at a higher level. Colleges and universities will benefit from having freshman classes already well versed and trained to accept responsibility for their learning.[1]

So who stands to potentially lose by these changes? Teachers and educators ill-prepared to navigate student-centered learning systems; teachers and administrators who can't be blamed for only knowing one way to implement while acknowledging there could be many ways; and those men and women who were only trained in traditional teaching systems. And even if they were introduced to distinctively diverse methodologies, these were not trained in an aggressive manner. Or worse, after being trained, getting into the field and classroom, and finding the busyness and business of managing students, they fell back on old systems that provided comfort and they were forgiven for doing so.

When the transformation occurs and the systemic change is no longer seen as different or new, teachers stand to lose. Not because someone is picking on them or bullying them. These teachers won't be victims of the tired, mistaken argument that once again no one understands them or really knows what they do and how hard it is. No, many teachers will just become victims of their own inability to remember that educators have to keep learning. We've allowed teachers to believe they had learned all they ever needed to know with the occasional professional development session thrown in every year just to keep the cycle going.

THE STAGES OF CHANGE

Watching the changes as they slowly start taking hold, there is a luxury of being able to decide, to choose whether the changes will occur on my campus or in my classroom. In many ways, the word *choice* isn't just something available for parents in the world of education reform. At this point, the word *choice* is afforded as an option for classroom teachers and building principals. But it's a slippery slope again.

Change is a funny creature, a slow-growing but exponentially more prevalent reality once systems start down that road. While there have been successful delays, deflections, and distractions thrown in the path of systemic change in education for over fifty years, the emergence and traction of the digital environment the students of today and tomorrow have known, those obstacles and barriers will disappear soon. Legislation, adopted practice, and common sense will eventually prevail and the traditional factory model will not be allowed to linger around in classrooms that truly value and respect the learner in a digital world.

Even now, what prevents the changes is often simply an illogical idea that we should not implement the changes simply for the sake of the teacher. And that will soon be seen as increasingly wrong. When this happens, and the full scale systemic change occurs in the practice and methodology across our nation, teachers who refuse to let go will lose. Their choice option will go away.

Up until now, it was okay to state that any student who needed personalized opportunity and self-directed curriculum was labeled as alternative and for kids who couldn't learn the way a person should learn. That will change and it will change in a big way. On that day, teachers who cannot teach in a personalized methodology designed to give students self-directed opportunity will be seen as alternative, as teachers who "don't get it" and can't teach the way a person should teach. And they will be left behind.

When change begins, in the early stages, it's often risky change. It's debated vigorously and cautiously. It's typically only adopted by those known as outliers. It's seen as alternative. But it soon becomes created change, intentional because it's beginning to catch on. The benefits of the change can be proven and there's a lot of understanding that some will choose it. In other words, that change is chosen. It's no longer considered risky and experimental. People have a right to choose it and are not ostracized for doing so. During that phase, though, practitioners are the ones with the choice and that's where we find many in education now.

But there's a third and fourth stage. The next stage becomes an adopted change. This is still seen as mostly isolated and optional, but notice is taking place that starts to question the usual way of doing things. The isolated changes start looking better to a broad population and people start questioning why the change doesn't replace the traditional. The change takes on a competitive edge and the two systems will go head to head. And the change has an agenda: to become adopted and seen as the best for those interested or involved.

The final stage of change will be a forced change with no barriers or obstacles. This will become legislative in nature and policy by practice. The change will be mandated and forced on teachers. And just as students have been forced to participate in a teaching system that didn't respond to learners, once the change occurs, teachers will then become the ones finding themselves forced to participate in learning systems that will be unforgiving should they persist in their resistance to change with it. The change will be systemic and those who can't find themselves in this will be left behind.

So lean back and take a deep breath because I understand that these may sound like harsh words. And I certainly know they can be offensive. It feels like a slap in the face to everything teachers have stood for. Separate from the emotional aspect of this. The world has changed and learners have changed. I understand that some will argue that students and their basic qualities won't change. And at the basic level, that's true. But the world has changed. And it's their world of learning. So even if it's hard, even if it's difficult, it doesn't change the fact that if we have truly given ourselves to a life dedicated to making sure learners learn and kids are changed, we have to pay attention.

What did we commit ourselves to anyway? To a methodology? To a system? To a practice? No, we committed ourselves to making sure kids learn. And in the digital world, that will demand a difference.

The issue is how we've defined teaching. Teaching is not delivering content. In the traditional system, the teacher is viewed as the deliverer of content, the most intelligent person in the room who decides when, how, and how much of a subject's content to articulate, give out, and deliver during each segment (each day) to students. That's a teacher. A very confining definition.

THE TASKS OF TEACHING

There are so many busy administrative tasks that accompany that definition, though. So let's take these task by task.

Lesson planning. This is a large chunk of time spent planning the presentation. During the lesson planning, there is no engagement with the learner, just planning the presentation and organizing the day's delivery of the content.

Lesson preparation. This is a large chunk of time spent preparing and getting everything together to accomplish the planning for the day's presentation of the content. Again, no engagement with the learner, just preparation.

Lesson presentation. This is done within the time frame when students are sitting before us: the presentation of the content, the culmination of those large chunks of time spent planning and preparing. The content is delivered to the group and there's not a lot of genuine, personalized engagement with individual learners. It's a class thing, a group dynamic.

Assigning the work to reinforce the content. This is an administrative piece that should help the group of learners deepen what they've been taught. Once again, no personalized engagement with a learner. The assignments are another group dynamic.

Assessing the work to measure performance on the assignment. This is a student-by-student assessment to see how each scores on the assignment. There is no engagement with the learner, as this is supposed to be objective. For reasons discussed elsewhere, this sometimes isn't possible, but the nature of assessing work should be that it's objective. But still, the engagement with the learner isn't evident.

Grading the assignment. This is task heavy and time consuming. Some would say this is the same as assessment, but it isn't. Grades become the most subjective result of assessments and it's unfair to give this the heightened sense of sacredness it's never deserved. And as is typical, there is no engagement with the learner.

Providing feedback to the learner that helps them improve. Sadly, this often becomes something that seems to be a choice for teachers. The amount of feedback can be absent or outside of the expectations of some teachers. The excuse is that a teacher cannot be expected to seriously give such a time-consuming task too much attention, especially if that one task steals so much time from the other supposedly important tasks it takes to be a real teacher. Oh by the way, this task is defined by a true authentic engagement with every learner.

It seems there's a pattern here. Maybe it's simplified too much, but think about the definition of teaching. First, if we say that the definition of a teacher is the sole possessor of content who delivers that content, we have to know one important thing: technology can do it better. Though it's sad to say, even a simple computer can deliver content better than a teacher. Delivery is delivery. Delivery doesn't engage. It only delivers. So let's get over that as our definition of teaching.

Second, if we take each of the busy tasks detailing our definition of teaching, we have to recognize the pattern. As we tick off each item on our list, we see it. In each task, there is no real engagement with a learner. There is no engagement with a student. There is work. There is busyness. But no engagement.

If we would just take the time to look hard at the emerging world of digital technology, we would have to admit one unavoidable truth: technology, powerful now and more powerful in the future, can perform each one of those tasks better than a teacher, more efficiently and more accurately, and faster, more precise, and more effectively than a teacher. Technology can even perform a diagnosis of a student on a daily basis quickly and accurately, something rarely even done in classrooms except on a pop quiz. Technology can place a student in an individualized plan quickly and accurately based on the diagnostics.

The tyranny of administrative busyness and bureaucracy that we have successfully wrapped into the work of a teacher has stolen our understanding of what we should be doing for kids, except in one area: *feedback that improves the learner*. This is a teacher spending time with a student, personally and genuinely providing the understanding of how the student can do better and be better.

Motivation is a key to learning. If a kid sits in the classroom and has no motivation, extrinsic or intrinsic, it really doesn't matter what we do. The kid won't learn. Engagement is a key to learning. Buy the books, line them up in rows, and make them sit up and pay attention. If they don't engage, they won't learn. They may show up and they may even "pass" our class. But that doesn't mean they've learned.

We have gone too far in our definition of "teaching" and made it something it isn't meant to be. We've morphed the idea of teaching into something akin to university professorships that start at the top of the heap with Ivy League "old school" lecturers and then scale down to the high school (and even elementary school) levels. This, and only (or mostly) this, is teaching: subject matter experts that prepare their presentation and deliver it each day to enraptured students. That's the pure idea and "teaching," wherever we are, tries to get as close to that as possible. If we *do* that, we have done our job. That's the visual we get when "teaching" is mentioned.

Thinking about engagement, one typically arrives at the conclusion that we need to find ways to engage the student with the content or material needing to be learned. Yet in an industrial age system of education, where the job of "teaching" can be accomplished by performing the tasks of "teaching" as defined by that system, engagement means much more than student to content.

If it's defined as the pure idea of lecturer and subject-driven interaction, it's easy. What's hard is engagement—true engagement for each student. No computer ever motivated someone to do more and be more. No software program ever inspired someone to stretch intellectually.

But we often just have disengaged teachers. And it's not that they intentionally disengage from students. They just don't have the time. Technology cannot replace teachers because empirical evidence shows that an engaged adult passing knowledge and wisdom to younger generations has always been a hallmark of successful learning. But we have to start utilizing technology in ways that get us away from this tired, wrong, and crippling idea that "teaching" is primarily delivering content, lecturing, and verbally offering our volumes of information to students.

Technology can personally diagnose, prescribe, and deliver content to groups of individuals better than humans. Technology should be used to replace the Industrial Age elements of education. Why? Because we need those who have committed their lives to changing the world through their work in the classroom to be free to engage with every single student in the classroom.

It's not a matter of replacing teachers with technology. It's a matter of leveraging technology to do what it does best. So a teacher can do what they should do best: engage with a kid and motivate, encourage, and be the change and growth agent for that child. That's legacy living. We have the opportunity to do it now more than ever.

So what should the twenty-first-century educator be doing? It may be best to approach the primary responsibilities for educators from a conceptual framework. While the factory model of schooling allowed the tasks of educating students to be wrapped inside a packaged "work" concept, the demands of the twenty-first century must be met through a results paradigm. Previously, the measurement of results for good education has looked to the completion of work-related to-do lists where administrators and teachers could simply check off the list each day.

In a high-stakes testing and accountability world, we just tested the kids at the same time on the same things, thinking that would give us a true measurement of whether the to-do lists had accomplished the goal for learning. One doesn't have to look too hard at the system to know that this doesn't really tell us much.

THE BUSYNESS

We have adults with a genuine desire to help kids. We have students with a genuine need to learn. So we put these students in buildings where they outnumber us and we place these adults in that same building to make learning happen. We create an organized factory process and require the learners to fit within the process. And the adults do what they can. But life-changing connections between the adults and students are minimal at best because the system isn't made for that.

The adults can successfully connect with a few students, but the more difficult connections won't happen because the system keeps everything moving. The adults feel frustrated, or at the very least should feel frustrated. And most students learn how to navigate the system. We end up with reluctant learners, missed opportunities, and diminished capacity to really benefit from the best the teacher can offer for every learner. Yet graduation night comes and we hand the diploma to every stage walker and send them down the line.

Meanwhile, the community outside that building keeps telling us that we have to measure results. But that becomes a moving target because we don't know what to measure. So we look to that test. And from that, we judge schools, teachers, administrators, and districts on whether they are good at what they do. Honestly, if the teaching system we have is all we have, any educator can perform the to-do list, but that doesn't mean learning happens. Kids can perform well on a test, but that doesn't mean learning happens.

We've created the cycle. The public screams that teachers don't know what they're doing and they're hurting our kids. So we spend enormous amounts of funding to develop tests that are supposed to give us some measure of comfort that "if a child can pass this test, then you can sleep tonight because this test will tell us whether a child's teacher is good."

Then we tell our teachers that the test is coming. And we tell our kids the test is coming. And our campuses and classrooms become preparation centers for that test, until parents and policymakers realize that the test takers and the test preparers are working in test preparation centers. Then the public screams that the test preparers don't know what they're doing and they're hurting our kids. "They're teaching to the test!"

Thankfully, we got there just in time and put a stop to it before they did too much damage to our kids. We slap them on the back of their hand and tell them to get back to teaching and this time they better know that we will be watching them much closer now that we know they've been doing nothing but getting the test takers ready for the test prepared by people we don't know but trust for some reason. So the test takers look to the test preparers, and there's a collective understanding that the test is coming, but we can't actually say anything about it or do anything about it. But if we do, don't mention it at home.

Everybody's nervous. The parent is nervous. The principal is nervous. The superintendent is nervous. The teacher is nervous. The kid is nervous. All because of that test that somehow gives us a sense of comfort.

The day approaches and our teachers have to secretly prepare kids for that test. All of us trust that we can finally identify those bad teachers among us; we can once and for all know whether that building I'm sending my kid to is a good decision or not. We can get rid of that teacher and sleep at night. And it's going to be a fair process and a level playing field because we stepped in just in time when we got suspicious that the teacher, alone with my kid and his or her friends, was doing nothing but getting him or her and his or her friends ready for the test.

The day finally arrives. And on the same day at the same time, we walk them into the room and put that test, prepared by people we don't know but trust for some reason, in front of every kid. And we turn the hourglass over and the sand starts flowing. The kids are on the clock. Every kid. Every single kid. Every last one of them.

Thankfully, we've made stringent rules for this. The teacher can't say the wrong thing because that will ruin the magic powers of that test and turn it back to what it was before we gave it those powers and make it just another piece of paper like any ordinary piece of paper. Don't say this or do that. Don't do this or say that. This is our day to finally bring those teachers out into the light. This is our time when we can finally confirm what we've feared all along. This has to be done right. And if we give the same test to every kid, we can finally know whether that teacher belongs in that room with our children. And the sand keeps running.

The kids, every last one of them, finish the test and we lock them away safely until we can turn them over to the authorities. They are gathered and mailed under strict guidelines to protect the magic. And we wait.

The tests are calculated. And the day arrives to announce to the town how we did. The percentage games kick in. Everybody knows the percentages. If we can only fail a certain percentage of our learners, we've done our job. Parents and principals wait. Teachers worry. They wonder if they were able to prepare a sufficient percentage of the kids in the classroom to be ready for the magic test without getting caught at making sure a sufficient percentage of kids were being prepared for the test.

The scores come out. Everybody's calculator comes out. And the news comes out. Hopefully, this time, the truth will come out. We can know once and for all whether that adult belongs in that classroom. And maybe we can do something about it. The power of that piece of paper will tell us.

The funny thing is that, on the day when those scores are returned and we see how the kids did on that test, there never seems to be a lot of surprises. There's rarely any instance of kids we believed were going to do well actually failing that test. We do see many students we feared would fail actually do better than we thought they would. But the individual results are never headline-grabbing news stories. We don't have any network pieces shown on the six o'clock news that evening featuring a kid that everybody thought would tank the test that actually surprised the townspeople and passed with flying colors.

Those kids we thought would struggle with the test struggled with the test. And those kids we thought would blow the top off the test blew the top off the test. That's when the explaining begins. Well, we knew this one would have problems because this one has this situation at home or this situation in life. But wait. Wasn't this test magic? Hold everything. Didn't you tell us this was going to finally tell us whether that teacher could keep working at our school? We thought the test could give us peace about whether our kids were learning. Can we or can we not trust the magic of the test? Do we have a valid and reliable measurement to determine whether that's a bad teacher or a good teacher?

That's when the logic takes over. That's when we have to patiently explain that we could have probably predicted that this child or that child was going to struggle because of their particular circumstance. Surely you didn't think that we could develop the same test and give it to every kid on the same day and turn the hourglass over with same amount of sand and expect that process to give us something that was going to surprise us. Did you really believe that was going to tell us anything different?

So knowing that, for the sake of a level playing field, we gave the test across the board to every kid, we put calculation measures in that are supposed to make room for certain groups of learners. We legislate or levy rules and scoring measurements that require a PhD to interpret and understand, all in the name of working on the percentages. Get the percentage of failures down to an acceptable level.

If only we can get that percentage down below the line, we can put the billboard up and place the banner by the entryway of the school. It's funny that the banner never says "Our school is a great school because we only failed 20 percent of our children last year." Meanwhile, back at the office, we start the phone calls. We have to make sure we let the parent know their child is a failure.

Thankfully, though, we now have a way to get rid of the bad teacher. And next year, when every one of the teachers is in every one of the classrooms, just as it was the year before, we can at least now be comforted by the fact that we have been able to confirm that we have those bad teachers in our midst. And nothing changes. But at least we had another good year filled with plenty of excitement and anxiety.

Somewhere in the middle of all this is a child, a kid growing up and learning something. Or nothing. Or everything. We're not sure because we are way too busy with our testing process to actually be engaged with anything other than making sure we get it all done on time. Did we mention it's a cycle? We work hard to make sure we don't change it. We may tweak it a little and we may work on pieces and parts of it. But we don't change it in any transformative way.

The cycle of standardized mandated high-stakes testing should stop. Now some might say this takes us back to the point in history where we realized that we needed a way to know that our kids were sufficiently prepared, not only for graduation but for life.

The workforce was telling us our kids weren't ready to take their place in the job market. Colleges were having to remediate too much. Studies were proclaiming that we weren't competitive.[2] And faced with all that, we didn't implement change in what we were fundamentally doing in our classrooms. Instead we just developed a system to test our system. We started bringing in high-stakes testing. And the cycle began.

We needed to know if a student progressed through our teaching system, would that student still have to be remediated after high school? Would that student be able to compete? Would they be able to jump in the middle of a job market? So we tested the system. We didn't change the school calendar. We just shoved the testing system into the teaching system. And here we are, still going through the cycle while knowing the system isn't really changing the competitive edge and not knowing how to address the fundamental issues that caused the cycle in the first place.

Some are going to argue that if we remove the testing cycle from the teaching system, we will never know if we have done our job. How can we be sure students have successfully achieved what they should achieve?

If we don't change our teaching system to a mastery-based learning system, we may not be able to now. The matter has to do with how we define success. In years past, students were getting passing scores and credits without actually knowing content and information. Left to the subjective and well-intentioned human teacher, it can happen. Even now, how many students can "pass" a class but not "pass" the test? So if we do not change the teaching system, we may have no hope of ever changing the testing system.

However, if we create the mastery system, letting students master content and prove it on objective mastery exams at the end of the units and courses, there's no need for the test. We don't need to look at the percentages to get a comfort level with the lowest number of failures on that test to determine whether this is a good teacher.

We don't need to schedule all our kids on a timed, same day, same test platform to evaluate a teacher. The student doesn't progress unless they master. And the progress mark is 90 percent. Meanwhile, if we design the day that allows personalized learning, objectively testing it systemically, we can create the capacity to prepare, engage, and educate kids on worthwhile things that will make a difference once they leave us.

This testing system isn't some evolution of an increasingly improved process that has gotten better over time so that if we remove it, we go back thirty years. It was an answer that deflected and turned us in a direction that, frankly, at that time may have been the best option we had. But that was then.

Today, we can actually address the concerns from thirty years ago. It will mean we have to transform the system, though. So getting to the heart of it doesn't mean we tweak what we have. It doesn't mean we analyze how to make it fit because we certainly can't go backward. What it means is that we stop and bring those issues back to the table in the light of current resources and opportunities for teaching and learning.

It means we have to ask ourselves, had we had these resources thirty years ago, what would we have done? And it means we have to change the system. The testing system got us through those thirty years, but we can now leave it and move to a mastery system that does a better job for learning and provides us with better opportunities to motivate and engage learners.

ALL THAT MATTERS

In education, all that matters is motivation and engagement. A motivated adult engaging with a motivated learner will be successful every time. This is why we see so much success in true homeschool paradigms where a parent engaged with their child ends up doing a better job than the local high school.

In our factory system, we have a huge population of disengaged students who have learned our system and reluctantly comply with it in order to finally leave it behind one day and get on with real life.[3] And we have passionate adults, wanting to do so much more for kids, relegated to a disrespectful role of factory workers checking off their lists and looking for those rare opportunities to connect when time allows. Meanwhile, the system keeps moving along.

Across our nation each morning, that door closes. Close to two hundred days each year, our children are sitting in classrooms, having been dropped off, delivered, or otherwise brought to these classrooms for the purpose of learning. And every morning, that door closes. These children are now in the hands of an adult. That's the long and short of it.

The majority of educators today have successfully navigated their college years and certification requirements without once being asked, "Do you love kids?" Now the majority of educators today actually do love kids, but the absence of the intentional, confrontational question is a factor in a steady decline of teacher engagement and self-efficacy as they increase in years of experience in the field. The question doesn't get lost in the noise and busyness. The question is never asked.

No element of human relationships is more crucial than love. No characteristic of interactions between all of us is more vital than love. Yet we don't talk about it when we're preparing our teachers. We talk about being relevant, being professional, and being organized. We ask them to study the history, the theory, and the practice. But rarely, if ever, are they confronted with the question, "Do you love kids?"

So let's look at the conceptual framework for educators in the twenty-first century. In its most simplistic form, we have to start seeing administrators as architects. Designing a learning system, as opposed to a teaching system, will require administrators to see their role as being more than managers of large populations of kids. They must begin seeing themselves as architects, skilled in design and intelligent thought. Architects have to create the framework for the environment. Architects have to deploy their resources in a way that connects the teacher with the student, every student.

And teachers? What should a teacher be doing in the twenty-first century? For lack of a better term to define the role, a teacher should be a shepherd. There's no way to avoid it. At the end of the day, if an adult has been given twenty-five students, that teacher is responsible for the entire group. And it should stop being a percentage game where we just shoot for an acceptable percentage of success. The teacher has to apply their skills in a way that connects with each individual, not twelve of the twenty-five. That's not possible in the traditional model.

A teacher is a shepherd with the responsibility of making sure everyone in their charge receives everything they can provide. Later, we will look at how this is possible, but for now, we have to address how the teacher should conceptually approach the classroom.

In this framework, the shepherd doesn't herd content and organize the content, spending the majority of the time on the curriculum. The shepherd herds kids, learners. The shepherd watches over the student, monitoring and watching over the progress of each as they learn. We already have isolated systems where this is being done and we can make it happen systemically if we begin to define our role in a more engaged fashion.

If we design our learning systems, leveraging the best we can provide through technology and the best we can provide through engaged teachers, the learner thrives. The models of encurricular learning can be replicated in a way that transforms our classrooms into centers where teachers connect and students progress.

THE ALTITUDE OF TEACHING

In some ways, the role of the teacher can be compared to the concept of flight. A teacher should be able to monitor students applying correct and intelligent monitoring to each individual. The technology can perform the tasks and the busy work of lesson planning, presentation, placement, assessing, and grading. *But the teacher has that human element that cannot be replaced.* And if the technology is used correctly, the teacher finally has the time to engage with every learner.

So back to the flight plan. A teacher will sometimes fill the role of shepherd from the vantage point of a satellite. Some students just don't need as much focused attention. They know how to learn. They thrive because they just seem to be able to progress even without us. And if we free them up to progress at their own pace, they do fine. We have to watch and we have to provide feedback. But that feedback may be at a lower level of intensity. We just have to watch and engage when necessary to help them when needed. Like a global positioning satellite, we can give them direction when necessary. But that just seems to be all they need. They know how to get there.

Some students will require more. For those students, we become more like a pilot of a passenger airliner. We have to provide more focused attention and the feedback should be more frequent and intentional. We have to guide and instruct them in a more direct manner. That's okay because these students will be fine if we can be just a little more hands-on in our interactions.

Some students, though, need us to be crop dusters. We have to fly low over these learners because they need more help. They have the ability to learn, but we have to fly at a lower altitude over them to keep them moving. We measure their progress, using the technology available. We schedule more time to provide feedback and direction. In other words, we have to provide more support at ground level to see them succeed. That's also okay because, if we use the technology correctly, we have the time and capacity to do so.

The model we will look at later in this book is an encurricular learning system that can give administrators the opportunity to be architects and teachers the opportunity to be shepherds. And it can be done systemically.

THE DIFFERENCE BETWEEN *SHARING* INFORMATION AND *TEACHING* WISDOM

One important point that has to be accepted for this to work is that in a learning environment, we never teach content. We only share content. Once that content is shared, the learner decides whether it will be learned. And that only happens if the learner wants to be engaged. That drives home the fact that motivation and engagement are the variables of true learning.

We don't teach information, we only share it. Technology can do a better job at sharing information than we can. So what do we teach? The answer is simple: we teach, or should be teaching, wisdom or the ability to grow and mature. This twenty-first-century world is sharing content consistently. But is anyone really connecting with our kids to help them mature?

We have left the development of wisdom behind for most students because the busyness of our teaching system doesn't give us the time to engage with every learner. So they reluctantly learn and we stay frustrated because we don't have the time to engage. If we can connect, we can motivate. If we motivate, they will stay engaged with the process. Even the best teacher will only have enough room to truly connect with a small number of kids. There will always be that cool teacher that everyone likes.

Connected is engagement, being in the middle of what that kid needs or where that student is in their journey every day. And that's hard to do. In the teaching system, it's virtually impossible to do. But in a learning system, it's not only possible, it's probable. It's probable because you've finally freed an adult to be what they wanted to be when they wanted to be a teacher.

You've burned away the busyness of the delivery system and handed the tasks over to the technology. A computer cannot connect with a person. An app cannot create a relationship with a student in a caring way. But we have countless numbers of teachers doing this every day. And if we free them from the tasks more easily performed by the technology anyway, and we push, train, and encourage those teachers to engage with every learner because we've now given them the freedom to do that, we will have our best days ahead of us.

In the proposed model, as well as in other models, the teacher can engage with learners because the teacher now has the time. The technology hasn't replaced the teacher. The technology is leveraged to free the teacher to do what teachers should do.

Teach wisdom. Sharing information takes so much time, but technology can do it effectively for each individual in a way that each individual needs. And the learner can progress. But the learner now has a teacher with the time to teach the most important elements of growth and maturity. Let the technology share the information. Let the learner progress faster or slower as necessary. Don't impede the learner. But the teacher is now able to connect, engaging with every student, providing feedback and interaction.

It's understood that many teachers may think they already do this. And there are those individuals who do know how to engage more easily and broadly than others. But in the twenty-first century, using the technology and the teacher intelligently, we can create opportunity systemically, across the entire campus, where the idea of "bad teacher" and "good teacher" is no longer a factor. We can provide a systemic model where every learner has the opportunity to progress according to their specific need and ability. We can minimize the dangers of students being left behind and abandoned at worst or frustrated and reluctant at best.

No teacher left behind. It should, and can, be our greatest day. Just as the emergence of technology has changed our world in so many areas, the day when that change transforms our education system is now happening. And it will happen systemically in our immediate future.

Hopefully, as we learn how to create the needed systems throughout our national framework of schools, we can see a better role for teachers, a higher role for administrators, and a greater opportunity for students. Architects and satellites, former presenters of information, become shepherds for every kid. It's not only possible but probable. But we have to be intelligent and we have to be determined to make it happen.

SUMMARY THOUGHTS

- Motivation and engagement are the keys to learning.
- Technology can successfully and effectively perform all tasks of teaching except the most important: providing genuine feedback to each learner.
- In the encurricular learning system, teachers have the time and capacity to engage with each learner.
- Administrators should develop a paradigm of an educational architect to design learning environments on the campus.
- Teachers are shepherds over their students.
- Teachers in the encurricular learning system engage with students by determining the balance of freedom and structure each student needs.

NOTES

1. D. Sparks and N. Malkus, *First-Year Undergraduate Remedial Course-taking: 1999–2000, 2003–04, and 2007–08* (Washington, D.C.: American Institute for Research, 2013).

2. D. Kelly, H. Xie, C. W. Nord, F. Jenkins, J. Y. Chan, and D. Kastberg, *Performance of U.S. 15-Year-Old Students in Mathematics, Science, and Reading Literacy in an International Context: First Look at PISA 2012 (NCES 2014-024)*, U.S. Department of Education (Washington, D.C.: National Center for Education Statistics, 2013).

3. P. C. Schlechty, *Engaging Students: The Next Level of Working on the Work* (San Francisco, CA: Jossey-Bass, 2011).

Chapter 6

WHAT MUST HAPPEN NOW

DOC'S STORY: "ARE YOU IN THERE?"

My wife and I raised three sons. Each was different and each was the same in so many ways. As a young dad, I was busy trying to figure out how to conquer the world and make the car payment each month. And as a dad who wanted to make sure my boys knew I loved them, I always tried to make sure they received the attention that growing children need from parents. But as attentive as I tried to be, sometimes I was so busy even when home. And when one of them would come in to show me the latest picture he had drawn or tell me the story of his day, I would, as parents often do, give a cursory nod or "yeah, that's great, buddy." Now it's not that I wasn't interested. But we just get busy.

Well, it always worked. Until it didn't. One of the boys figured it out at a very early age. When he would show me that picture, he would stand there with it and watch my face, my eyes. He was waiting. Giving the verbal acknowledgment wasn't good enough for him. Nodding my head while still attending to whatever task was at hand wasn't going to work with this one. He would stand there watching me, my face, my eyes. He wanted my attention. Not just my words and nods. He needed to know that I was engaged. He needed to know my attention and encouragement was genuine. Only when I dropped what I was doing, stopped what I was doing, and focused my full attention on the drawing would he be satisfied. Only when I commented on something that proved I was actually paying attention would he be happy and move on to his next adventure.

To achieve the shift in our paradigms in education requires change. And anyone standing close to this universe of teaching and learning hears the word *change* all the time. We exist in a culture of change. But this shift requires changing the right things the right way.

With a managed teaching system model, it becomes too easy and convenient to assign blame, label bad, and make excuses. However, this isn't about good teachers or bad teachers. Nor is it about graduates or dropouts. It's about learning. Progressively learning and being engaged with learning our entire lives. That's not a technical piece of a puzzle. It's a paradigm. And it's not just our students who need this; it's our educators.

This shift will most likely be better achieved if we focus on our generations of educators rather than our generations of students. We have heard terms, language, and labels used to identify the generations of students growing up in a digital world. And we have seen the dividing lines drawn between those in that world versus those who came before it. But the transformation of education is coming and we must focus on our greatest opportunity now: our teachers.

For the purpose of this chapter, we can simplify the distinction by identifying two types of educators. Though individuals have varying interests and competencies related to digital environments, we would be best served by identifying these types in a broad manner, choosing to distinguish these types as "generations" of educators. One caution is that these are often defined by age groups. However, rather than being that simple, these generations are probably better defined through elements of their exposure, adoption, and trust in digital capacity.

GENERATIONS OF EDUCATORS

First, we have Emerging Generations of educators. The Emergent Educator was most likely taught in traditional systems while attending K–12, wanted to be an educator as a career, and was trained in the established system of teacher training and preparation. The certification is held, the job is secured, and the classroom is assigned. The Emergent knows the power of technology and uses it in every aspect of life. There is potential and there are exciting days ahead. The Emergent Educator is valuable.

Second, we have the Experienced Generations of educators. The Experienced Educator has been in the trenches and knows the realities of that classroom door opening and students filing in. The traditional system is considered trustworthy and reliable. While technology is great, it doesn't change the fact that kids are kids. The Experienced feels a tremendous sense of responsibility. The Experienced Educator is valuable.

The Emerging Generations see the disconnect between teaching systems and learning systems, but feel their greatest risk may be in straying too far from their training, forgetting the classroom lesson planning, and depending too much on individual student empowerment. Can the classroom really be controlled and managed if students actually have too much freedom to direct their own learning? And if not, will that Emergent be held responsible for this lack of control and loss of organized group progress, with its accepted percentages of success and failure?

The Experienced Generations see the disconnect between teaching systems and learning systems, but feel their greatest risk may be in trusting technology too much while abandoning what has proven to be a somewhat reliable, organized system for the sake of being relevant. Even with the liabilities of the traditional system, there is at least some sense of safety there that gives some relative assurance that the process doesn't become unmanageable. The Experienced Generations may often feel they are being asked to give up too much ground.

The Emergent Generations use the "gold" of technology while the Experienced Generations have to continually dig for that gold. It's hard work. Every new device, program, and application is a new discovery or revelation to the Experienced Generation. To the Emergent, it's just an upgrade.

Students in the twenty-first century are different and the education system will transform to a new paradigm for teaching and learning. But getting there will require the generations of educators to change more dramatically than just adding computers to the classroom. It will require changing how we "think."

Marrying these two generations of educators is difficult. One can't expect that simply turning over all control to students will transform anything. However, one cannot expect that the organized management of a teaching system will have much capacity in the future. A shift in paradigms is needed.

So what are those major paradigms we must reshape? The arguments could be endless. However, for our purposes, we will focus on three major shifts that must happen in our thinking now.

RESHAPING HOW WE TRAIN AND CERTIFY EDUCATORS

So what must happen now? There are many pieces to this and they can seem scattered and disconnected at times. However, if we focus on the one most important element first and drive each piece through that, we can experience transformation. *The single greatest shift we will need is to dramatically change the way we train, prepare, and certify our educators on a national level.*

While this may seem simple at first glance, it has layers of significance that often remain ignored. The educator is an apprentice while being trained. In our schools of education and our state agencies assigned to certify the trained apprentice, we continue training the traditional systems and practice. There will be small pieces of genuine attempts to include technology and digital environments, but the primary role and responsibility for teachers is still based on the twentieth-century teaching system. We continue teaching our lesson plans.

Unless we see permanent shifts in our thinking at the training and certification levels, we will not transform our education nationally. Rather than training the traditional teaching system, we have to educate ourselves at the highest levels, the legislative and agency levels, on twenty-first-century learning systems and how we can create the cultural shift in our thinking. If we train the apprentice in twentieth-century traditional practice, and ask the apprentice to trust that practice, the Emerging Generations will continue filling our vacant teaching positions with hesitancy to empower the student.

We have been satisfied with our training and trusting of our certification. And we want the Emerging Generations to use whatever tools they can to help students. But a shift in the paradigm creates a foundation of understanding for these generations as they move out to our schools. It gives them a better handle on what has to be accomplished.

That foundation can only be created at the most solid level, the level where the apprentice is asking to be trained.

Our schools of education should begin an intentional, serious effort to rethink how we train the apprentice. Rather than adding a technology course to the program, we should be filtering all teacher training courses through a digital technology platform. Rather than teaching an isolated credit for technology utilization, everything we train should be created and employed for the purpose of ensuring the apprentice is an engaged learning systems educator.

Let's be clear on some points. We are not talking about technology courses, though they may be a part of what we want. We are talking about teacher engagement courses.

Transforming doesn't happen unless the cultural understanding changes. Cultural understanding doesn't occur unless thought (the idea) changes. But as we've stated often, thinking is good, but only implementation matters. So how can we implement the change in our training and certification?

It starts with the leaders of our schools of education. It starts at the most effective level, the credit courses necessary for the degree. We still require traditional practice courses in order to attain the degree for teaching. This can be changed, not added to or modified, but changed.

It doesn't require technology experts. It doesn't require only the younger generations among us. It requires those educators who have the capacity to see the digital world and its consuming environments while also keeping the balance of what education should be doing. Remember the crucial elements of progress measurement and mastery learning and how these can define our purpose.

In our courses of study as apprentices, we can be exposed to the four determinants. We have to begin studying the elements of content delivery in the twenty-first century, not as a supplement but as the foundation for leveraging what is available. Rather than establishing the lesson plan model and daily presentation of content, we should take advantage of the dynamics of the "skilled craftsman to apprentice" relationship to teach our teachers how to teach, and what that means, in the twenty-first century.

Our schools of education are led by those who have the greatest opportunity to shift our paradigms successfully. But those educators have to understand that the K–12 classroom, which may be far removed from anything they've done in years, is different now and will be even more different soon. These school of education leaders must create training that is relevant to the world of the new learner.

If we have trained the apprentice wrong, and the apprentice uses the training when things threaten to become unmanageable, we have done nothing to help change things for kids in future generations. Leaders on the higher education level may believe they are preparing tomorrow's teachers, but what they are actually doing is preparing the teachers for many days *after* tomorrow. If our higher education leadership would create training and preparation congruent with the new learner rather than propping up an outdated system of teaching, we would experience a shift in our paradigm.

Bringing an acceptable status to digital delivery of content in the classroom, and giving it the integrity and credibility it deserves, will be the greatest building block for our future training and preparation. And not bringing this cultural shift to the forefront of our training and preparation will continue delaying transformation and be the major dysfunction experienced by generations of educators.

Those working within the educational realm seem to know there's some give and take on the concept of "direct instruction." We just understand that no one ever admits that a strict, regimented definition of lecture-driven "direction instruction" is acceptable any more. Of course, we mix it up in the classroom. Why yes, we get the students to work together and use the computers.

Those of us in education just know that when we say "direct instruction," we don't necessarily mean "direct" instruction, that is, the spoken word reading of lesson content and additional verbal sharing of the day's lesson from the instructor to the students in a group setting. In other words, the lecture. We educators know that this is not what we mean when we say "direct instruction." *But the world doesn't know that.*

The world looks to us to help structure their own paradigms for what they see when they see a high school graduate. There are many entities beyond the halls of the high school that offer opportunities, and have requirements for, our students once they graduate: military recruitment, college athletics, and industry. These entities are not K–12 environments. Yet they need to set the parameters for inclusion or approval when students seek to engage with their work. Scholarships, assignments, and future opportunities are part of these entities.

Not being K–12 environments, these entities look to us to define what is meant by "direct instruction." And there is no give-and-take understanding with these entities. Needing to set the standard for approving membership when students apply after graduation, or even during their high school years, these entities don't use an ambiguous measurement for direct instruction. "Direct" means direct, and direct instruction means verbalized content presented to students by teachers, out loud, hands-on, and ears up, presented and delivered by the teacher in the classroom. We can change that paradigm for these organizations.

RESHAPING HOW AND WHY WE DIAGNOSE AND TEST STUDENTS

Standardized testing, at least in the form currently used, has to be eliminated. Measuring the progress of the individual student has become competitive and used only for the purpose of measuring schools. While knowing that some students will not achieve the passing score, educators have to focus on getting the percentages to the acceptable level for the campus and the district. This diminishes the significance of the engaged educator with students.

If we continue standardizing a testing system that establishes a false success rate for students based on the ability of every individual to pass the test the same way on the same day, we will continue experiencing the growing environment of disengagement. No one wants to abandon all forms of measurement. What and how we measure, however, is most significant.

To help us understand this role of diagnostic testing, we need only consider the same role in a medical field. The different perspectives and purposes of testing can be summed up in two words common to this field: biopsy and autopsy. Similar comparisons in the field of education have been used before,[1] but, for our purposes, we will be targeting the paradigm of testing as it currently stands in our education system today.

A doctor who suspects that a patient may have a medical issue routinely schedules that person for a procedure to gather information related to the issue. Examination of that area, or specimen, taken from the patient will provide the medical professionals with the data and understanding of the patient's current status and condition. This is a biopsy, *a test for the purpose of diagnosing the current condition and creating a strategy to address the issues identified from that test.*

It's done, hopefully, at the earliest stage possible. It's performed with a purpose in mind. Take a sample, examine the sample, and develop the plan. This is to prevent further damage, stop progress of harmful elements, and bring the patient back to a healthy condition.

Let's look at another test. When a person passes away, often an examiner will gather information and inspect conditions that possibly caused the death to determine what happened. This is an autopsy. *It's performed after it's too late to do anything about the condition*. There's nothing anyone can do.

Both are tests. And both are diagnostic tests. Yet the purpose and potential for both are vastly different. There is a huge difference between a biopsy and an autopsy.

Testing the way we do is more like an autopsy. We've tried to calculate what the test will ask, we prepare while being warned not to prepare, and we run the test in a standardized way for every unique student expecting standardized results. And we panic when it doesn't. We determine it's a bad teacher and a bad school and a bad district. It's an autopsy to see what happened. It's a "post" test. We should see testing as a biopsy, the "pre" test to see where the students are at the beginning.

To standardize a test for every student on the same day, at the same time, in the same way, is effective only if it's a biopsy, at the beginning, in order to assess the condition, the deficiencies, and develop the plan at the beginning of the year. *And we should remove standardization beyond that point.*

We currently run the test at the end, after it's too late. Our autopsy testing is done to tell us what happened. Biopsy testing can tell what can happen if we will only do these things. Some might think we perform biopsy testing because of all the penalties, warnings, letters to parents, federal money, and probations currently thrown in after the fact. However, it's obvious it isn't working. We do not run diagnostic testing that helps the individual learner.

Nationally, standards-based autopsy testing needs to become a thing of the past. Yet we must still be measuring the progress of our students. And mastery-based learning is the key to our measurement. This will demand a lot from us. It requires that we create the system where self-directed learning can happen.

RESHAPING HOW WE VIEW LEARNING AND TEACHING SYSTEMS

We have already addressed this concept enough. There are easily identified distinctions between a teaching system and a learning system. However, shifting our thought, thereby shifting our expectations for a classroom, will require that our very idea of what we mean by the word *educate* will need to change. It's important to know that admitting that we have teaching systems is not saying that these were bad or deficient. They were needed.

However, what we have to know is that it's not sustainable. And not just because of technology. It's not sustainable because learners are changing. Not necessarily because they want to change. And a teaching system that was vital in our past will not be sustainable for these changes in our future. This is not the way learners learn. *Changing our entire thought about what is meant by "educating students" is required.*

THE EFFECTS OF RESHAPING OUR PARADIGMS

If we can shift our thinking and redefine what we mean when we talk about schools, we can see some effects on significant elements of our education system. Some of these effects will be accepted gladly. Some may not.

There is the possibility that decision making from the bottom up may begin to lose its power. We have been satisfied for thirty years with an education system that considers a "tweak" to the school day a major disruptive innovation. We've been satisfied with an education system that throws out the statement, "How many kids have you taught?" and uses that as 1) a good reason not to trust proposed changes and 2) a strengthened reason to only allow change offered by trench warriors.

While we must always look to our educators as our greatest hope, we may not see a reshaping of paradigms on a national scale if we wait for the industry itself to restructure those things. Most people will see through personal viewfinders, "How will this affect me?" and too much change will cause too much concern. And thus far, there has been a lot of patience given because no one wants to propose a top-down decision-making world, especially if that top-down decision comes from those outside the industry.

However, parents, politicians, and policymakers feel just as great a responsibility to our children as teachers and administrators. "Hands-off" sounds nice. And it sounds right. But eventually, if delayed disruption continues, these individuals will become much more "hands-on." The luxury we have as educators to keep tweaking our ideas, rather than transforming our approach, can become a thing of the past.

There is also the hope that we can concretely connect the research with reality. Those most qualified to inform us on the research and what it says we must do for kids can be positioned at a field level to also inform us how to make it happen.

Rather than seeing our researchers as disconnected theorists, we can start expecting them to not only observe, but interact as well. Understand the hard job of the teacher. Don't just tell us what's wrong, but live among us to change it. Rather than seeing our workforce of educators as unenlightened outdated technicians, we can start expecting them to not just hear the research and shake the head, but implement as well. Understand that we don't know everything. Understand it's going to change, but why must it wait until we retire?

SUMMARY THOUGHTS

We must immediately begin a national effort to reshape the following paradigms:

- Reshape how we train and certify our educators.
- Reshape how we think about teaching and learning.
- Reshape how we test and diagnose learners.
- Testing in a mastery-based system eliminates standardized and post-testing nationally.

- Testing in the encurricular learning system will be defined by the following characteristics:
- Standardization occurs at the beginning rather than the end.
- Testing is used to diagnose and prescribe the student's learning path.
- Testing occurs through objective technology.
- The only post-testing in the encurricular learning system is the mastery exam.

NOTE

1. http://www.sciencedirect.com/science/article/pii/S0742051X10000466.

Chapter 7

THE TRANSFORMED SYSTEM

DOC'S STORY: "THE CONNECTION THAT MATTERS"

Across our nation each morning, that door closes. Close to two hundred days each year, our children are sitting in classrooms, having been dropped off, delivered, or otherwise brought to these classrooms for the purpose of learning. And every morning, that door closes. And these children are now in the hands of an adult. That's the long and short of it.

One of the best hours of my week is the hour I spend every Sunday morning. I have the privilege of teaching five year olds at my church. My wife and I volunteer for this because we believe that whatever we can do for preschoolers and their parents is time well invested.

Recently I was talking with our preschoolers about jobs. I asked them if they had any jobs. One child told the rest of the class that her job was to love her Mom and Dad. Immediately every child in the class agreed that their primary job was to love Mom and Dad.

Driving home that day, I thought about how cool it was to be in that time of life when you could confidently state that your greatest job is to love someone. Obviously, those kids just aren't mature enough to know that loving someone can't be your job. They're apparently not intelligent enough yet to know that loving someone can't be your first answer when asked "what is your job?"

Every morning, that door closes.

Throughout the year, I speak to many groups of teachers. As I consistently state, I love teachers. Often when I'm speaking, I'll ask them "What is your job?" The answers are textbook worthy.

Every morning, that door closes.

Oh I'm a firebrand when I do my job. I challenge anyone to match my capacity to get puffed up and pontificate. I can deliver a focused monologue on just what we are after out here. I can scramble and scurry around, busy and bothered. "What is my job?"

Every morning, that door closes.

The kid came back to the room after school one day to ask the teacher a question about the assignment for the following day. He didn't understand everything that had been discussed during class and he needed the teacher to go back over some of the lesson from that day. His request was met with, "I'm paid to teach it once. If you didn't get it, that's not my fault."

Every morning, that door closes.

I think that the majority of educators today have successfully navigated their college years and certification requirements without once being asked, "Do you love kids?" I also think that the majority of educators today actually do love kids, but the absence of the intentional, confrontational question is a factor in a steady decline of teacher engagement and self-efficacy as they increase in years of experience in the field. The question doesn't get lost in the noise and busyness. The question is never asked.

No element of human relationships is more crucial than love. No characteristic of interactions between all of us is more vital than love. Yet we don't talk about it when we're preparing our teachers. We talk about being relevant, being professional, and being organized. We ask them to study the history, the theory, and the practice. But at no time was I ever confronted with the question, "Do you love kids?"

We're afraid of it. Our society has created such a misshapen and uninformed paradigm of love that we filter the word and the concept through a clogged funnel of skewed perception and misunderstanding. And as sick as it is, there are evil people who should never be left alone with a child. Those extremes have damaged the ability of good people to even mention the word love *for children. It creeps us out. And that's the greatest injustice forced upon those good and honorable people who do belong in those classrooms, who should be teaching our children. They love kids, but it's difficult to express it in this day of predators who lurk at the edges of our worst fears. I hesitate to even give a sincere compliment to young parents about their children in a public place because it just causes red flags. So we neutralize the concept of love.*

And every morning, that door closes.

So I visited the elementary school tonight that will be the start of a new chapter for us. My oldest grandchild will start kindergarten this year. The other five will follow in the next few years.

Right now, they believe what all preschoolers believe. "My job is to love." And she will walk into that classroom and sit there with all the others. Her personality has formed during these last five years. She doesn't analyze herself. She doesn't question why she prefers blue over red. She doesn't criticize herself for the smallest of things. She is who she is.

But over the next five years, her perception of who she is, that loop that talks to her, will begin speaking. That small voice. And what happens during these years will create the feedback on that loop. She's about to be sitting among others and left alone with an adult.

I've got open eyes here. Each of my grandchildren owns the whole of my heart. Each is a precious treasure. And the oldest will lead the way for the others. But like any five year old, she's not perfect. So Miss Teacher, please don't tell her that she's always right when she has to also understand that she could be wrong at times and she needs to know the difference. Please teach her manners, respect, and honor for honorable things. Please teach her about hard work and being kind. Please teach her to be resilient. Please teach her to never lose the wonder of learning new things.

So many jobs, so many pay checks. All in the name of education. Grown-ups, saving the world.

But very soon, on a late summer morning, that door will close. And nothing out here will matter. It will be you and her.

So Miss Teacher, you have my permission to love my granddaughter. May you know that as your job.

The transformed education system will not be an apocalyptic terror that abandons what we have always wanted for our generations of children. But neither will it be an apologetic tweaking of the traditional systems where you won't even recognize the change at all. It will move education reform from an interruption of the traditional to the systemic and complete disruption that's been staged to launch since 1985.[1]

Many of the terms, ideas, and perceptions we have in education are based on how we structured the teaching system. Those concepts limit our understanding of what we do and how we do it. The thinking may be that we would have to abandon those foundational concepts in a way that removes the anchors of good education. And that can make one anxious and uncertain about whether a complete transformation is our best move.

However, these anchors aren't being removed. Our foundations won't be abandoned. But they will, and should, be changed. It's a matter of redefining what these terms and ideas mean in the transformed learning system. And redefining these will not be the gateway to the transformation. Rather, the new definitions will just become a part of the language and understanding once the transformation occurs.

"BEST IDEA" OR "BEST PRACTICE"?

As it currently stands, the experiments continue to be isolated and disconnected. It remains that way because it's not systemic. At this juncture, it's everyone's best idea and quickest response to innovation. So there's a lot of "best idea" experiments where everyone comes to see what you're doing. Then a lot of effort is placed on replicating your "best idea" with their particular modifications. It now becomes their "better than best idea." That's innovation from the bottom up, at the lowest level. And it works if we don't focus on transformation. It's what happens if we don't transform our paradigm, our thinking.

That's why the transformation will have to come from the top-down. To transform will require a broad scope. The transformation must have a wide view. The top-down has a legislative nature that hovers over all our districts and systems. We've developed this "best practice" paradigm that staves off any real change to the system. As soon as we think the changes, the innovations, or new ways start getting too close to the established classroom, we play the "best practice" card. It works because it keeps those not in classrooms at bay.

After all, surely only those who are at that field level know what's best. And the "best practice" strategy works every time. So if there has to be some form of innovation, some response to the calls for change, keep it simple, keep it localized, and keep it isolated. Let's try that new idea. Let's replicate that cool model over there.

And we create our version of the "best idea." We've created a national radar screen of "best ideas." And none of it threatens "best practice." And the "best practice" is understood to be the teacher-controlled, organized, and managed teaching system. *Redefining what we mean when we say "best practice" is crucial.*

This will change the "best idea" paradigm to a "best practice" implementation.

ALTERNATIVE EDUCATION

In the teaching system, we have been given the benefit of claiming that anything outside the controlled, teacher-centered classroom is alternative. It isn't the norm. It's for those kids who can't survive in the teaching system, paced to a classroom speed and scheduled to begin and end together. If a student can't function or perform well in that environment, the student needs an alternative option. And those "alternatives" are endless. But those alternatives are necessary because those students just don't "get it"

It's flipped after the transformation. Once the student-centered learning systems become the norm, the standard, the definition of "alternative," will be changed. Rather than looking at the student who needs an "alternative" environment, it will become the teacher who will be seen as an educator who can't successfully navigate learning systems. It will be the teacher who must teach "the old way" in a classroom that can be controlled and managed by the adult rather than the individual learners.

Sadly, this can be hurtful for an educator to be labeled this way. It can be hurtful to know that you have the ability, the capacity, and the potential, but you're now considered "alternative." And you are limited to only one framework, one choice for what you do. It won't be fair to have the label of "alternative" assigned to you as an educator simply because you don't fit in the accepted structure of the transformed system. To do this to our most passionate and professional adults, who are with our children every day, is unfair.

And that's where the reality will hit close to home. Is this not what we've been doing to learners for years in the traditional teaching system? They've been capable, they've had potential. Yet because they don't function well in that controlled, paced system, we give them the label, we brand them with this identification of "alternative," and we make them feel less because of it. Sadly, in the transformed system, it may be the teachers who won't "get it."

So how do we head this off? How do we just get there without labeling anybody, teachers or learners? By understanding that the digital learning system will happen, it won't be alternative, and it will be the new paradigm. And start getting to it now, changing our training, redefining the concepts, and welcoming the shift. Get on board. Get ahead of the transformation and wait for it to catch up to your classroom.

Age doesn't matter and years of experience don't matter. Those of us born before the digital world was created aren't irrelevant or behind. In fact, we have crucial elements of wisdom and engagement for learning that will be needed, no matter what system is used. But if we do not understand the need to transform our classroom, and we stay entrenched in our teaching system, we will become the "alternative" ones.

DIRECT INSTRUCTION

The concept of direct instruction is one of the most often misunderstood elements of education. There's just some comfort in defining those two words, then combining those two words, that lends itself to a reliable, trusted process. "Instruction" is the channel of transferring knowledge and information. In other words, "teaching." "Direct" is the intimate, person-to-person interaction. The expert to the apprentice. The teacher to the student. So the idea of "direct instruction" leads us to believe that the human teacher is taking the responsibility to interact with the learner, person to person, to transfer the knowledge successfully. It's comforting.

The idea has become institutionalized so much that it has taken on a life of its own in our society. Those outside classrooms and campuses define direct instruction as simply as possible. Teachers verbalizing subject content to students. That's not the way we as educators understand it. But the concept was so institutionalized in the teaching system environments that those outside our framework go to that simple definition. So it's a matter of teaching those outside our framework.

Those in education understand direct instruction as the process where learning happens due to certain specific elements: engaged interaction with learners, goal setting, and organized sequence of assignments and content, assessments and reviews, opportunities for questions and explanations. These elements, fully controlled by the teacher in the teaching system of the past, can be realized and achieved in delivery systems designed around technology. Educators are necessary, but verbalizing content isn't the standard for encurricular learning systems.

We already know this. But we will have to teach other adults, those outside our circle, before we can expect a fair treatment and understanding for our students when they interact with those entities. Embedding the new definition of "direct instruction" culturally will have to occur.

TECHNOLOGY AS SUPPLEMENTAL

As we balance the role of the teacher and technology in our classrooms, we've always considered the human as the foundation, the go-to element. Technology has been considered supplemental to the instructional process. It's been seen as the "extra" and the "added." At the end of the day, if all else fails, we have the human. So having the technology is nice. But it's not the necessary.

That changes in the transformed encurricular learning system. The technology becomes the foundation. The teacher is the "value added" element. This in no way minimizes the significance of the teacher. *The role of the human being becomes even more significant in a system that is anchored in technology.*

It may be that we tend to minimize the word "supplement." We perceive the supplement as being something that is nice to have, but if we don't have it, we will be fine. However, this won't be the case in the encurricular system. We need the teacher. Though our students can learn all they should learn, though they will have access to any content, any information, in a technology delivery system, it means nothing without the engagement of a motivated educator. There's nothing insignificant or minimized about this.

However, in the transformed system, no longer will we think that the go-to standard is the teacher driving everything while technology will be a nice luxury if we can afford it. The technology will become the standard, but the teacher will be just as important, or even more important, than ever.

SELF-PACED

This term has been used for years to put a negative face on any curriculum or process that recognizes the individual learner. We've glorified the group learning systems to the point that we just believe that working and walking together in an organized, planned manner is the expectation. Any learner wanting something different needs to be in a "self-paced" environment. And "self-paced" makes you different from everybody else. So we call it "special" and we call it "self-paced" and it loses legitimacy.

Yet all of us are on a self-paced journey in our lives. There are times we have to accelerate what we do in our lives and jobs. All of life is self-paced. Why would we expect anything different from children and adolescents? We grow best, we learn more, when we are motivated. And we are motivated when we learn in a manner designed for our own strengths. We learn more when an educator has the time and the capacity to engage with us.

Learning should be personalized and looking down our noses at those brave enough to demand a self-paced education will become a thing of the past soon.

GRADE DESIGNATIONS

This one may be difficult. From small town America to our largest urban cities, we identify the current status and progress of the learner, particularly in high school, by the grade designation: freshmen, sophomores, juniors, and seniors. It tells us how far you've come and how far you have to go. And we can readily "calendar" that. If you're a sophomore, you'll be finished in May or June two years from now. Our curriculum is written that way, our funding is based on it, and our celebrations center around those designations.

In an encurricular learning system, that may go away. When we truly focus on the credits earned and the credits needed, we lose the schedule. It won't fit on the calendar. American life centers on that calendar. But that's no reason for delaying or preventing the transformed system. It just means the reshaping of the paradigm means to also reshape how we manage that calendar.

SUMMARIZING THE NEW PARADIGM

So it's best to provide a summary related to the transformed learning system environment and how the various elements act, react, or interact within that environment. How will it look?

Testing will be intentional and purposeful in the new paradigm. The temptation would be to state that testing goes away. But measurement has to occur. In the teaching system, we've known that standardized testing doesn't measure learning, though that seems to be the perception we prefer our public to have.

Any elements of testing in the new paradigm will measure progress. Testing will create an effective system of diagnostics and prescription. We will test for a reason. And we won't feel it necessary to apologize for testing. Once we place our focus on the reason for testing, to truly help the individual learner, we can use what we learn to position the student strategically on a better path for improvement. No greater tool than technology is already available for this and in the new learning system, we can leverage it effectively.

The key will be where in the process we demand standardization. As already stated, placing a standardized format at the beginning changes the reason for testing. We will learn to use results in a personalized way for the individual learner. Testing in the new system will be important. However, the politicizing, polarizing, and finger-pointing elements will no longer drive over something as important as measuring true learning in our children.

On a national scale, testing disappears as a political banner to win votes. We can focus on the kid once we understand the reason and purpose for why we test, how we test, and what we do once we've tested. Standardized post-tests disappear and mastery-based learning (and the measurement of progress for mastery-based learning) appears with the credibility and integrity it deserves.

This paradigm shift will also greatly affect districts. No more reasons to disguise our instruction to avoid detection of preparing students for that standardized day. No more fear of being accused of "teaching *to* a test." Instead, every district can proudly state they "teach *from* a test."

If we diagnose the learner, prescribe the path for improvement, and measure progress, it becomes the driving force behind every move we make. No one has to hide and no one has to pretend to ignore the test because the foundation for that improvement lies within the results for each child. It's to be expected that the place for learning will be the place for learning. And what will be learned is established through knowing what needs to be learned. What needs to be learned is easily determined at the beginning.

Districts can break away from the environment of merely trying to survive and focus on helping students thrive. Educators and students can work together. And once that prescribed journey begins each year, we will measure progress. For those lovers of testing, there will plenty of that embedded within curriculum. However, every test, rather than focused on the one-time performance, will be positioned to check for reviews and measure progress.

Districts can stop the experiments once we realize that it's not a magical formula or secret, yet-to-be discovered ingredient that we hope to stumble upon in this age of innovation. Rather, it's just the realization of finally being able to do what we knew we should do but we couldn't do because the tools hadn't been created yet. In the new system, we will realize true engagement between the educator and the ones we educate.

The new system will have cast off the burden of the former teaching system that demanded the bureaucratic, organized process and will allow districts to narrow their focus down to individuals. No more will a district wanting to break out of the standardized testing system, or even wanting to protest the standardized testing system, be seen as a rebel outlier, or worse, feel the threat of probations, violations, or sanctions.

District administrators can be architects, intelligent professionals free to use that intelligence to chart a path of learning rather than navigating a swamp of distracting and confusing rules and laws. These high-level educators can use their practiced skills of strategy to focus on the improvement of their kids instead of having to focus on how to beat the percentage game to avoid penalty. Educational architects understand their role as higher than playing the game each year and spend their valuable time structuring learning opportunities instead.

It's never been the cool thing we've needed, adorned with computers and apps. It's always been engagement over experiments. When the new system is established and the paradigm has shifted, the district architect is free to stop experimenting and focus on teaching educators the language of this system and leveraging the teachers and the tools.

That leads to the anchor, the technology. Since the day that computers first entered our lives, and subsequently our classrooms, we've seen a struggle that either places too much or too little emphasis on *the tool.* Why this happens is difficult to ascertain at times. There have always been new tools. And educators have always welcomed new tools that provide new opportunities.

Yet it seems that we've taken technology and formed an emotional attachment, or detachment, about it that minimizes the potential for our classrooms. We vilify it as something that shouldn't be trying to take the place of the teacher. We give it too much attention or we glorify it as the end all answer to our funding or personnel shortcomings.

In the new paradigm, technology sits at the right place, as a tool that should be utilized to its fullest potential. That potential is far greater than any tool we've had before. Technology will continue to be a culture-shaping, culture-changing element of the modern world. And as it continues to expand, its capacity for the instructional improvement of what we do on our campuses will expand as well.

In the encurricular system, we no longer merely *accept* technology. Rather, we *adopt* it as the anchor. We no longer tolerate it but celebrate it as the foundation for how to best educate all future generations. Human beings passing knowledge and information to human beings is education. And human beings create, manage, and use technology. Once we've matured past the emotional issue, we will be using it to do those diagnostic, prescriptive, delivery, and assessment tasks that encumbered the educator well into the twenty-first century. The new paradigm lays aside those debates and just simply demands the intelligent utilization.

Curriculum writers and providers will be highly engaged in two necessary aspects of the encurricular learning system. One is to intentionally develop curriculum in a scope and sequence that supports and enriches the learning environments. Two is to make it affordable. These companies won't be driving testing systems and will respond in an aggressive manner to make content accessible and affordable for learners, educators, parents, and stakeholders.

Parents will understand the mastery-based learning system. Just because it's simplified doesn't mean it's simple. It's rigorous and responsive to the learner. And parents can understand it. It's where the child is and where the child needs to go. There are no complex games of ratios and regulations. It's just learning. Some students will progress further because they need to go further. But every child learns and parents understand the system.

Training will drastically change in the new paradigm. There's no need to change our training if we believe that the teaching system is the prime environment for learning. If we believe that we've trained to improve learning, there's no need to change. However, if our goal is, as it should be, to prepare educators so they can function effectively in the adopted system of education, then the dramatic change in our training will take place. We successfully prepared teachers for the teaching system. We will now be preparing teachers for learning systems.

That training will have a center and a focus. The centerpiece of our training will be preparing educators for self-directed, mastery-based learning environments. Encurricular systems will require different training. No longer will we just acknowledge that we should be personalizing education, minimizing teacher-directed instruction, and guiding rather than controlling the learning process. *We'll actually train our teachers in those things.* Intentional, disciplined training that frees new educators, having grown up in a digital world, will now utilize those very things in the classroom.

The center will be the best practice understanding of the twenty-first century. However, our training will also be focused, a determined focus on engagement. Those who have entered education but have no concern about engaging with students, every student, will find it difficult to thrive in the encurricular learning system. Our training will focus on aspects of true engagement, even focusing on the greater calling for a teacher.

Quality focused engagement, those elements that create the best teacher-student relationships, will be a major part of our training. In the teaching system, it was possible to do the tasks of teaching, perform those job activities that were inherent to that system, and never actually engage with students. We taught it and left it to them to get it. We could teach but that didn't guarantee that learning happened.

Whether learning happens in the new paradigm will be much more acute and critical. In a mastery-based system where progress is measured, no student can hide behind a disengaged and noncaring shield. Their lack of engagement with their learning process will be evident.

Having technology performing so much of the busy work of the classroom will now clear the way for the educator to engage daily with the student. No student will be lost in the group formations of the past. Teachers will actually be able to teach, if they see teaching as something other than delivery of content. Teachers will be grateful for the fact that we've matured beyond the thought that the best they can do is something that can be done by even the simplest computer. Teachers invest themselves in students, every student.

We should give teachers the respect, the regard, and the credit they've long deserved. And that should not come only from within their own ranks or the small group of parents or students they have the time to influence each year in the teaching system. These elements of encouragement and gratitude should be shown to these professionals who have committed to our children.

Creating the encurricular learning environment will communicate to educators that we want them to invest in our children in an even greater way. We expect their best and we want those elements of engagement. Teachers are best positioned to have the greatest influence on every child and each child. The new paradigm allows that.

The greatest equation in the new paradigm will be the daily engagement of the educator to the individual student, a motivating engagement wherein the teacher is comfortable with the necessary elements of twenty-first-century education. Using technology intentionally to do those tasks formerly thought to be the primary "signs" of teaching. The teacher is comfortable with the learner being self-directed and empowered.

Empowerment. As we implement the changes that will occur once we have transformed to full student-centric learning systems, most likely the greatest shift will be seen in the idea of empowerment. This transfer of decision making will be difficult but necessary for teachers. Simply put, in the transformed learning system, there will be three primary equations that must be assessed and addressed each year and each day: 1) the amount of structure versus freedom required for each student; 2) the mixture/utilization of technology versus teacher for each classroom; and 3) the engagement altitude required of the teacher for each learner.

For each student in a learning system, there's no question that delivery, measurement, location, and time will define the classroom. But the equations listed here will become much of what teachers will do for each learner. The rising tide of technology and the transformation of education will require something from us that the old teaching system never asked of us.

We will hand off the decision-making power, in strategic ways, to our students. In other words, we will empower our students. In the new learning system, empowerment will be important. As the system becomes the way education looks, acts, and feels nationally, empowerment in the hands of learners will become natural and expected.

Our classrooms will be fields of learning where the educator calculates and measures the altitude of engagement for each learner. This will require that the teacher knows every child, not merely have the student in the class. The teacher will know the needs and strengths of every learner. The teacher will know the diagnostic results and the prescribed learning journey.

Most importantly, though, the teacher will love and care for every student. Some educators might believe that it's not possible to force anyone to feel this way about anyone. Our response to that will be, "Why not?" An adult not capable of that should not be in the classroom.

In the teaching system, countless numbers of educators have been able to actually do these things already. And they should be applauded for having the highest caliber of engagement even while working in a system that doesn't structure that. Those same teachers will welcome the change. Those teachers will be the ones who will lead the way for the generation of educators who will finally take us through the change. The new paradigm structures the learning environment so that it forces all teachers to be engaged and clearly identifies those who aren't.

There are skill sets for teaching in the encurricular learning system. We will teach educators how to diagnose and prescribe. We will teach educators how to measure learning. Most importantly, we will teach educators how to engage.

We've always known that the engagement of the teacher with a student is the ingredient for motivation and success. Teaching systems only allow educators the time and the freedom to blend in that ingredient on a limited basis. But if we've always known that quality engagement is the key element for student success, why have we not centered this, focused on this, in our training? Training the technical skills for a teaching system takes up too much room. In the new learning system, these quality engagement skills will drive our training. This is what changes learners and we will be able to give it our highest priority once we transform.

There are changes for teachers and students in the transformed system that will go beyond the classroom. In our teaching systems, we talked a lot about standards, but with the new paradigms, we will have better conversations about responsibility and ownership. The best teachers want to take ownership and responsibility for each student. That approach demands that we give them the freedom, time, and expectation to do this. The elements of responsibility and ownership will be just as important for students as well. And expecting students to have ownership and take responsibility will demand that we empower them in the classroom.

Balancing the equation between structure and freedom for each student requires us to know the student well. Larger rules, classroom expectations, will remain, but the structure/freedom equation is the foundation of engagement for each individual learner.

The teacher will determine the altitude of engagement for each student. Some students will navigate encurricular systems with a lot of freedom and little structure. Some will need the structure as they continue developing their capacity to handle the freedom. Self-directed will demand self-discipline and that equation is necessary. That equation opens the door for the teacher to be engaged daily.

There is much we will be able to do in the transformed education environment. The ability to structure apprenticeships and internships will benefit from learning systems that are no longer confined by the sectioned day, the rigid clock and calendar. Students will be better prepared for life after high school, whether it's moving to careers immediately after the diploma or entering colleges and universities. The university framework has the best position to change our training. Community colleges are our best opportunity to create those links between the high school and life after the diploma.

In education, we create a sense of a "pendulum swing" related to ideas and changes. We bring in our latest idea, implement and work it until it outlives its lifecycle of three years. And our entire system goes through the swinging of the pendulum on a large national scale periodically. We create a consuming environment that is now the answer until the pendulum swings back and we react to all the negative things that the last environment created. It's reactionary. All in the name of reform.

It's time to dismantle the pendulum, take it apart and create the new paradigms for learning and teaching. Become responsive rather than reactionary. Stop the projects and promises and reshape what we think when we think about education nationally. No more delays. We have all the pieces and all the intelligence to dismantle the pendulum. This generation of educators can be the significant generation that started the national shift.

That's responsive. That's transformation.

SUMMARY THOUGHTS

1. Change in education has already happened, but without realistic or broad implementation and there doesn't seem to be any real effort to create a systemic implementation in any form beyond isolated pockets and alternative options.
2. We are in danger of creating an "education reform" model adorned with computers and nice technology that doesn't actually disrupt practice, but merely supports the traditional teaching system.
3. There is a clear distinction between teaching systems that teach something and learning systems where students learn something.
4. We have teaching systems created in the last century that have successfully controlled education so effectively that we now believe that this is how people learn.

5. We will move to student-centered learning systems and educators unable to make the shift can, and will, be left behind.
6. Our current state is composed of three basic paradigms identified as a teaching system that can't respond to each learner further exacerbated by a testing system that doesn't provide effective measurement and an honest education reform system characterized by small experiments and pockets of promise that delay broad systemic transformation.
7. What will eventually break the industrial system will be the consuming digital generations that will not tolerate the old system any longer.
8. The one nonnegotiable item is that the system must experience transformative systemic change on a national scale that changes classroom practice in order to create sustainability in a world with emerging and expanding twenty-first-century resources.

NOTE

1. C. Christensen, C. W. Johnson, and M. B. Horn, *Disrupting Class: How Disruptive Innovation Will Change the Way the World Learns* (New York: McGraw-Hill, 2008).

Chapter 8

TRANSFORMING THE DISTRICT

Pea Ridge is a small community sitting eight miles northeast of the town of Bentonville, Arkansas. Small by most standards (a population of approximately 4,500), the flavor and culture in Pea Ridge are woven throughout the town and surrounding area. The largest Civil War battle west of the Mississippi was waged in the fields just outside the city limits and the drive to Eureka Springs in the Ozark Mountains can afford one an opportunity to stop at the local cafe for a Blackhawk burger. Speaking of the Blackhawks, everybody in town knows that the clock stops on Fridays nights in the fall when the team takes the field in the stadium to play their hearts out.

Though a small community in size, Pea Ridge is also greatly influenced by the presence of Walmart. Not the local store located in the heart of town, but the corporate offices just down the road in Bentonville. This is blue jean corporate America, infused with an understanding that what we do for kids is important and we should always do what's important.

The people in Pea Ridge may not be walking through Times Square on their way to work, but they most assuredly know they reside at the epicenter of the largest corporation in the nation. There's no sense of backward thinking or small town ways. Yet there's also no sense of entitlement or arrogance here. The population is clearly divided into two distinct groups: those who arrived here recently and those who have been here forever.

The school district is led by a dynamic superintendent named Rick Neal, a man with a heart for kids and a passion to do everything he can for those attending his campuses. Rick is committed to this district and isn't worried about the effects on his career trajectory in his decision making.

Mr. Neal worries about one thing: Are his kids getting as much as they possibly can from his teachers? Is the diploma he hands the graduates worth as much as possible for those young adults as they walk across the stage? Or will they struggle for the next two years as they try to navigate life, whether on a college campus or in the job market? Rick Neal wants what every superintendent wants for his graduates, or at least should want for graduates.

Local industries had talked with Mr. Neal often about the need to receive better prepared young men and women for the workforce. Though everyone knows that anyone fresh out of high school is going to start out at a low level in the job market, there shouldn't be a parenthesis in their lives while they patiently wait to build up enough experience in their job to gain credibility, skill, and exposure to the working life.

These industry leaders appreciated the efforts of the district. But it's costly and not the most optimum strategy to just expect that the best they were going to have entering the market, looking for a job, would be graduates with nothing but high school credits on the ledger. Could more be done earlier to help these new workers, maybe even giving them a head start, that eliminates that two-year process before they get up to speed and have to "learn on the job?" That's a huge deployment of resources and these local industries were wondering what the district might be able to do to help solve this equation.

Additionally, those attending college the next year needed much more. The University of Arkansas, the largest in the state, is located in Fayetteville, a half hour drive away. Most students head there and register for fall classes the year after graduation. There is a great responsibility felt in this small town to make sure that these students are well prepared and ready for higher education.

College isn't high school and the need to balance everything demands mature responsibility and elements of character that students may or may not have when they step on the university campus. Are they ready? The fact that they hold a high school transcript is not necessarily the indication or predictor of success. Can the high school do more?

As he listened and thought about these things, Rick Neal was certain of one thing. A traditional vocational school and college prep were not the answers. Or not the best answers. The high school consistently ranks in the top ten of the best high schools in Arkansas. Yet he knew they could do better.

Now. Throw all this right into the middle of the twenty-first century. Mr. Neal was very knowledgeable about the process of buying computers and placing these throughout the campus. While knowing that the technology had been good in some areas and merely adequate in others, he genuinely wondered if there was a better way. That's when the idea for an "ischool" began to take shape.

For the 2014–2015 school year, Rick formed a relationship with a nonprofit charter school system.[1] This system had been developing blended learning systems for years and had traditionally established their campuses as a choice and option for parents in communities. Free from traditional districts, yet held to strict accountability standards, these charter campuses were labs for educational design and had been able to challenge conventional thought and practice. Rick Neal wanted something different, something transformative.

He approached the state board to receive his own charter, but he explained that he would not be asking traditional educators to design and control the learning system for his students. The district would hold, and own, the charter, but the responsibility of designing and supervising the learning system would not be traditional district personnel. Rick was handing this off to those who could possibly do more for his kids. And the Pea Ridge Manufacturing and Business Academy was born.

The Academy opened its doors in August 2014. Students in the eleventh and twelfth grade could choose to attend the new school rather than the traditional high school. These students would be in credit courses in a morning or afternoon shift. During their shift, they would be in course work delivered through technology. Teachers were given a cohort of students to supervise and shepherd.

The students were involved in a Pathways program in the morning or afternoon determined by the shift they attended for credit courses. Morning shift students attended Pathways in the afternoon and afternoon shift students attended Pathways in the morning. Pathways is the half-day student training, certification, and workforce program specifically designed for the campus. This program is created to partner with local industries to prepare students for careers after high school. High-level courses in sales and logistics, medical training, welding, and media arts are available. Students receive direct instruction in classes and training connected with careers linked with industries in the northwest Arkansas region.

During the time spent time in Pathways, students will be involved in training from personnel in those industries and will gain experience through internships and apprenticeships. At the conclusion of the program, students will achieve certifications and additional licenses that offer opportunities to enter the workforce much better prepared.

Pathways is the dream that Rick Neal had always had for his graduates: the ability to enter college with more college hours and the opportunity to enter the workforce at a more advanced level. Making the connections with industry had to be more than vocational education. It had to be separated from a traditional track-oriented high school day.

And how to schedule this would be virtually impossible unless he went outside conventional thought and approach. Students would have to be able to spend the required time in credit courses, but the structure of the day and the deployment of teaching staff would have to be different.

When you visit the academy, located in its own building to the south of the high school, you'll notice the differences immediately. Charley Clark, appointed from within the district to be the first director for the campus, is an energetic young man with a genuine passion for students. He and his team have been trained differently and have implemented a blended learning system that sets the school apart from anything else in the district. In the beginning stages, students in the final two years of high school can choose to attend the academy. Rather than being considered "alternative," the district has gone to great lengths to communicate that the academy is a school of distinction where learning and teaching looks and acts different.

The following is the step-by-step process for the learning system.

THE PLAN AND THE PROCESS

Each student is in a cohort group supervised by an assigned teacher. These teachers are responsible for ensuring that their students are progressing in their learning. Charley and his team employed a learning system that used the elements much like the modern GPS system for trip navigation. The system is articulated in this manner:

When one uses a GPS system, there are three major components: the driver, the vehicle, and the satellite. In conventional teaching systems, the driver has always been the teacher, making the decisions about the content, how it's delivered and when, what subjects receive what focus, and how much content is to be given to the learner each day.

In the system used by the staff at Pea Ridge, they developed the theme, "Give the Kid the Wheel." In this system, the vehicle is the curriculum and content to get to the destination. The student is the driver making the decisions each day on what, how much, and how long each subject is focused on throughout the learning time. The teacher is the satellite. In this role, teachers monitor the progress of their students consistently.

The teachers are subject matter experts, but they don't prepare and present lesson plans. However, they are not mere facilitators just making sure computers are running. They are highly engaged with their cohort, providing constant instructional support when needed, mentoring and counseling each student along the way.

The system is designed that students must achieve a 90 percent to progress to new levels of learning, so grading is not a task that teachers perform unless the subject is in an area, such as specific language arts, that requires subjective interactive assessments. Students work to earn the right to take mastery-based exams. The following is the training process used to prepare teachers for the system.

KNOWLEDGE INQUIRY

Knowledge Inquiry is a learning experience to find answers and information using strategies and available tools.

1. The student receives the Knowledge Unit from the Cohort Teacher.
2. The student is required to complete all question sections for Social Study Knowledge Units. The student is required to work chronologically through all Mathematics Knowledge Units. In other Knowledge Units, the student is allowed to answer only the three quizzes and the Unit Practice test.
3. The student can study the content in the Knowledge Unit, answering the questions as he or she progresses.
4. The student can scan the content in the Knowledge Unit, finding the key words and phrases in the questions and then finding the answers in the book.
5. The student can search the Internet using the computer and find the answers with search engines.
6. The student will have access to high-level learning resources such as instructional videos, teaching tools, and targeted assistance in specific learning areas to use individually and repeatedly as necessary.
7. Once the student has completed the Knowledge Unit, the unit is submitted to the Grading Area. The student begins working on another course Knowledge Unit immediately.
8. When the Knowledge Unit is graded, the student will need to correct any incorrect answers.

ACCURACY is the goal.
STRATEGY is the process.

KNOWLEDGE ANALYSIS

The purpose of *Knowledge Analysis* is to put the learner in a learning experience to organize and think about new information while connecting the knowledge to his or her life.

1. The student will meet with the Cohort Teacher and define two to three research topics from the Knowledge Unit.
2. The student will study and research these topics as a systems thinker, answering the following for each topic:

3. *What is it? Clearly identify what you are researching.*
4. *What is its system? The topic is part of a whole system. Define the system.*
5. *What role does it fill in the system?*
6. *Why does it matter? Why should we care?*
7. Your research should prove that the student understands the content from the Knowledge Unit.
8. Give the student guidelines on written, oral, and creative presentations.

UNDERSTANDING is the goal.
CREATIVITY is the process.

THE ORAL DEFENSE AND THE MASTERY-BASED EXAMINATION

The purpose of *Mastery* is to ensure that the student knows the content, is able to express knowledge, and achieve success on objective tests.

1. Once the research is complete, the student will schedule an Oral Defense with the Cohort Teacher.
2. The Oral Defense is a ten to fifteen minute dialogue with the Cohort Teacher to express understanding of the Knowledge Unit.
3. The Oral Defense is not one of the two to three Knowledge Analysis topics, but is an overall verbal presentation of the student's learning and understanding.
4. If given approval, the student will schedule the Mastery Exam for the Knowledge Unit.
5. The student must score 90 percent on the exam to be allowed to progress to the next Knowledge Unit.

ACHIEVEMENT is the goal.
STUDY is the process.

At this point, the student has accurately found information and worked to achieve complete mastery when allowed to use tools and even work with other students, conducted research, completed projects as a systems thinker to learn new knowledge at a deeper level (converting into information into knowledge), expressed and articulated understanding to a teacher, and earned the approval and the right to take a high-stakes objective examination with high expectations for mastery that will allow the student to move forward in the learning experience if successful.

In most of the learning system subjects, the grading will be as follows:

1. The student will take the Mastery Exam once all research tasks have been completed.
2. The student will be scored on the Mastery Exam for the Knowledge Unit.
3. If the grade is 90 or above, the student will be allowed to progress to the next unit.
4. The 90 or above score will be recorded in the school record system as is.
5. If the grade is below 90, the student will be required to complete additional work in the Knowledge Unit and schedule a second testing.
6. The student will be scored on the second testing.
7. If the score on the second testing is 90 or above, the student will be allowed to progress to the next unit, but the second score can only be recorded as a 90.
8. The second score (90) and first score will be averaged together.
9. The average of the scores will be recorded in the school record system.
10. If the score on the second testing is below 90, the actual score will be recorded as a second grade on the unit.
11. The student will be required to study the unit and schedule a third Mastery Exam.
12. If the score on the third testing is 90 or above, the student will be allowed to progress to the next unit, but the third score can only be recorded as an 80.
13. The third score (80) and the second score will be averaged with the first score.
14. The average of the scores will be recorded in the school record system.

15. If the score on the third testing is below 90, the actual score will be recorded as a third grade on the unit. The student will follow steps 11 through 14 for all subsequent scorings until an actual score of 90 or above is achieved on the Mastery Exam.
16. Tests may be modified on third and subsequent attempts by eliminating questions already mastered.

Mathematics

1. Every student will be enrolled in a math course and will spend a minimum of forty-five minutes per day learning math.
2. The student will meet with the Cohort Teacher to discuss objectives for the Knowledge Unit.
3. Students must work systematically through the entire Knowledge Unit.
4. Student will be required to show progress to the Cohort Teacher every second day. The Cohort Teacher will initial and date the progress point.
5. The student will request a review from the Cohort Teacher at the end of each quiz.
6. The Cohort Teacher will review the Knowledge Unit and return the document to the student with any incorrect answers marked. The student will be required to make corrections before progressing to the next section.
7. When the final Unit Quiz has been completed and corrected, the student will schedule the Practice Test Review and the Mastery Exam with the Cohort Teacher.
8. The student will take the Unit Practice Test and submit it to the Cohort Teacher.
9. The Cohort Teacher will return the Unit Practice Test to the student with incorrect answers marked.
10. The student will correct and submit the Unit Practice Test.
11. Once the Unit Practice test has been corrected to 100 percent, the student will be allowed to take the Mastery Exam.
12. The student will be scored on the Mastery Exam for the Knowledge Unit.
13. If the grade is 90 or above, the student will be allowed to progress to the next unit.

14. The 90 or above score will be recorded in the school record system as is.
15. If the grade is below 90, the student will be required to complete additional work assigned by the Cohort Teacher and schedule a second testing.
16. The student will be scored on the second testing.
17. If the score on the second testing is 90 or above, the student will be allowed to progress to the next unit, but the second score can only be recorded as a 90.
18. The second score (90) and first score will be averaged together.
19. The average of the scores will be recorded in the school record system.
20. If the score on the second testing is below 90, the actual score will be recorded as a second grade on the unit.
21. The student will be required to study the unit and schedule a third Mastery Exam.
22. If the score on the third testing is 90 or above, the student will be allowed to progress to the next unit, but the third score can only be recorded as an 80.
23. The third score (80) and the second score (90) will be averaged with the first score.
24. The average of the scores will be recorded in the school record system.
25. If the score on the third testing is below 90, the actual score will be recorded as a third grade on the unit.
26. The student will follow steps 21 through 25 for all subsequent scorings until an actual score of 90 or above is achieved on the Mastery Exam.

HOW THE FOUR DETERMINANTS OPERATE

Any system designed to be a twenty-first-century student-centered learning environment must address the four determinants. The system being used at Pea Ridge addresses each of these according to the following.

Time

Rick Neal and Charley Clark knew there was more they could provide their graduates on commencement. However, they knew it had to address the real issues presented to them by industry leaders in the area. And they knew it wasn't the traditional vo-tech options forced into the school day. College prep courses, AP, and vocational education offerings were already available.

They knew they needed to create a Pathways program that was able to eliminate the typical two-year orientation and preparation period graduates faced immediately after graduation night. That Pathways program would take a legitimate half-day to be successful and it was the driving force behind the academy. But to have the time capacity to do Pathways properly, they knew they needed to change the learning system. Time was the key element for what they needed to do.

The academy addresses the time factor in significant ways. The students are in two shifts, morning and afternoon. The morning shift students are in Pathways until noon and in the academy learning system in the afternoon. The afternoon shift is in the learning system for credit courses in the morning and Pathways after lunch.

Because the learning system does not control the day, the students are able to complete course requirements and master all they need to know for their diploma. However, they receive a tremendous advantage (leveraging the time element) at the academy because they are allowed to move into areas that engage and motivate them, and upon completion of the final two years of high school they are better prepared for the next step in their journey.

The second aspect of the time determinant is the learning methodology itself. The system does not hold students back from progressing in their studies. Most students have confirmed that their greatest frustration in traditional classrooms was having to keep pace and go slower through studies so that classes moved together. They knew they could do more, but would disengage because of the frustration and, though successful in the classroom, they were, at best, reluctant learners.

These students always ranked at the top of their class anyway. They just wanted freedom to control the pace. And some students were frustrated because they needed more time on some areas and subjects.

These students found that the forced pace of a traditional classroom was no longer a factor once they enrolled in the academy.

The third way in which the time determinant is addressed is in being able to clearly define and draw the distinctions between the required learning for credit courses for the diploma and the time that can now be reserved solely for Pathways, the value added portion of the day. There is no time when the credit course achievement is discounted or minimized. No one wants to say that this isn't important. However, at this point in the journey, there are some things that can be done that bring more value to the diploma and can better prepare these graduates for life ahead.

Because the lines between the learning system for credit courses and Pathways are not blurred, the actual time needed for each is very focused and distinct. The learning system is not subject to the maddening complexities of high school scheduling with its sensitive and frustrating variables of getting every block of class periods right between teachers, times, rooms, and subjects. Anyone experienced in trying to get these variables to line up knows how difficult this is each year.

At the academy, there is a morning shift, a block of time carved out for learning in credit courses. This is a defined block of time set aside to meet the state requirements for credit course learning. This leaves the remainder of the day for Pathways. There is a clear focus for each.

Lastly, and probably most importantly, the academy addresses the time determinant with the freedom offered by blended learning opportunity. The ability to engage with learning can happen at any time. This can be on weekends, during holidays, and even on snow days. Students can engage with their courses at any time. The accessibility of the courses, and genuine progress in the courses, can be at any time allowed by the staff. This is an example of a blended environment that trusts the learner and knows that the barrier of time can be eliminated in twenty-first-century learning.

Location

The academy is housed in current district buildings. When searching for a suitable location for the learning center, leadership utilized the building used as a shelter for severe weather. This building was already sitting behind the traditional high school facility.

The building had no interior walls so the district laid out a plan where technology-based delivery and encurricular learning could occur. The ceiling and roof of the building are two stories tall, so the walls were built at nine feet, leaving open space above each wall. The learning spaces were created to comfortably accommodate thirty students sitting in various configurations.

Upon entering the academy, one is able to stand in the central open area and see each learning center. Furniture in the open areas and learning centers is diverse and is chosen to encourage students to work together. Students are allowed to work together or alone. Rather than being a loosely organized arrangement, however, the academy is structured intentionally to keep students engaged and motivated.

The Pathways courses are taught in other areas of the campus. These areas are dedicated to the innovative "industry-connected" portions of the school day. Medical, business, entrepreneurial, and technical industries are closely tied to the campus.

While most might believe that the campus has created another vocational-technical school, the emphasis that the district places on the right thing brings the opportunities to something far beyond traditional vo-tech. The key is how the school approaches credit achievement for students.

In most educational efforts such as this, districts have developed their programs, but then forced them into the traditional structure of the conventional teaching system. The credit courses are fixed related to the elements of time, location, and delivery method. However, the academy at Pea Ridge created the paradigm wherein the learning system was effective but not restrictive to these elements. Therefore students can keep moving forward in achieving their credits toward graduation, but the pieces of their learning committed to the Pathways program are not hurt in order to accommodate the credit courses.

Location for learning has become a nonfactor for students. While there are two shifts, morning and afternoon, in which students are in the learning center and content learning is occurring, the students are not solely confined to that location. Management and monitoring of learners still has to happen simply because it's a high school and high schools must be managed. But this management doesn't define learning. Learning happens where students have access to the content.

Measurement

As described previously, how students are measured for progress is high level at the academy. Students can work together and can seek assistance from teachers and others. Achieving a proficient level for the content learning is organized. And each student is monitored by an assigned cohort teacher. Not having to move forward in a group fashion allows each learner to progress and prepare individuals for the mastery exam.

Once the student completes the content for each unit of the course, the oral defense is scheduled. This is the point where the cohort teacher becomes much more intentional in assessing the proficiency and readiness of the student to attempt the mastery exam. The student will present the material, respond to the questions presented by the teacher, and submit any assigned projects or items required from the unit.

The oral defense allows the teacher to assess readiness, discuss the unit with the student, and determine whether the student is ready to attempt the exam. If so, the exam is scheduled. This exam is given to the specific student in the exam room. Once taken, the mastery exam is graded objectively. The academy students must achieve 90 percent on each exam.

The district and the academy must still take state assessments. These high-stakes tests are still administered, assessed, and accountable to the rules and policies set forth by the department of education. However, the learning opportunities for Pea Ridge students have been freed from the confining, restrictive elements of the traditional system.

Delivery

The delivery system for content ends up being the most misunderstand element for innovation. While the argument focuses on technology, and whether the role of teachers is or isn't significant and necessary in a technology-based system, the presence of technology is not the defining proof of twenty-first-century learning environments. Too often, technology just to satisfy the growing pressure of the masses only serves to buy time and delay transformation while only supporting the very systems that need the transformation. Technology is crucial. However, it isn't the only delivery system for encurricular learning systems.

At the academy, students are engaged in content learning during the assigned morning or afternoon shifts. This is focused and regulated to meet state requirements. Students set their goals each day and move forward independently. The curriculum is proprietary and written to support an organized, encurricular learning system. It's delivered through the use of laptops and mobile devices that students use during the shift times.

There is no classroom teacher and there are no group lesson plans. The technology-based curriculum is written to support the encurricular system to give students a comprehensive learning opportunity for each subject. Sectioned into units of study, the curriculum provides reviews, pre-testing, post-testing, and mastery exams. Students may be sitting around conference tables together, but each individual learner is engaged with their own study and progress.

At times, students may work together and may collaborate on projects. This is encouraged, as the learning system is designed to allow students to move forward within their particular capacity and skill level. Subjective grading does not happen. Once the unit is fully completed, the delivery system changes from technology to teacher. The cohort teacher, monitoring the student's progress throughout, now has the opportunity to hear the oral defense and assess readiness for the mastery exam. This allows the teacher to check for understanding and guide the student in areas where more learning needs to occur.

This delivery focuses the teacher on the individual student, focuses the engagement on actual need, and increases the effective preparation the student must have for the mastery exam. Rather than using technology as a showpiece that gives the appearance of innovation, the academy utilizes an intelligent blend of teacher and technology that doesn't hinder progress and ensures greater understanding for the learner once the system is fully complete for each unit.

THE GREATEST DISTINCTION

As stated often, there are countless innovative schools nationally. It is almost a requirement that a district, charter, or private school echo the education reform refrain accepted now in our journey. Many might say that the academy at Pea Ridge is simply another isolated experiment that proves the superintendent is forward thinking. On the surface, this could be easily stated and generally supported. What makes this different?

The district in Pea Ridge has one major distinction that separates it from others. It would be easy to show the campus off, tout the attraction and accomplishments, while also keeping the traditional high school secure and in place. However, this isn't the goal of the district. Rather than being an isolated experiment for a small portion of students, the academy is the first step in a district-wide transformation. Pea Ridge hasn't committed to encurricular learning systems solely for those upper high school students who choose the academy. The district wants all learners moving to encurricular learning systems by the time credit courses become important. This will be realized in a five-year initiative.

Doing this requires a much earlier focus on engaging students and teachers. Early elementary students must start focusing on the right things. To succeed in the encurricular system will require an increased capacity in literacy and reading comprehension. While keeping the infrastructure for elementary in place, Pea Ridge will be shifting the focus to literacy development, language acquisition, and comprehension strategies in elementary grades that provide opportunities for reading success much earlier for students.

Along with this, though, teachers will be incorporating character elements that combine self-efficacy and independence, but also cooperative learning. Students will learn from an early age to take responsibility for their learning through independent progress for success, but work together cooperatively for content learning. An observer might not notice the disruption initially. However, the focus is on how, what, and why the teachers will do what they do at this stage.

In the later elementary years, students will start taking assigned independent courses designed to introduce the concept of self-directed learning and expose them to the elements required for success outside a teacher-directed environment. Close monitoring by teachers will remain in place and characteristics necessary for this learning system will be emphasized throughout the day. Teachers will work closely with learners during this time, utilizing the professional development they receive and applying engagement principles to ensure students learn to work independently while achieving adequate progress.

By the middle school years, students have been exposed to the self-directed environment. Having received focused literacy instruction at the earliest opportunity in their journey, their capacity to thrive in an independent environment will increase their ability to be immersed more fully in encurricular learning systems.

At this point, students will be involved in required independent learning in a minimum of two subjects. These courses will be determined by the district and will provide a balanced offering of teacher-direct and student-centered instruction. As students work through the courses, greater focus will be placed on their effectiveness as an independent learner. Their success in this will be the mark of their preparedness for credit courses in high school.

Once students reach the level for credit courses, typically at the high school level, the major portion of their school day will be spent in encurricular learning systems. Courses will be delivered through technology and teachers will be engaged with students in a manner that supports and enriches the relationships necessary for individual student success. In that first year of credit courses delivered through encurricular systems, the academy will encompass the entire high school. When the district achieves the full implementation of the new learning system, every student will be involved in a progressive twenty-first-century opportunity.

In most situations, when presented with difficult tasks, initiatives, or risk, people will take one of two positions. Many will begin developing and articulating all the reasons *it can't be done*. Much energy and effort is spent explaining why it just won't work. However, others look at these same changes and begin developing and articulating *how it will get done*. Yes, it will be difficult and different. And the risks are understood. But that doesn't prevent it from being accomplished once the challenge is met.

The district at Pea Ridge is composed of those in the latter category. There is an understanding that, rather than continuing to protect and entrench the traditional, the district has started down the road toward full transformation. The infrastructure of the district, the professionalism of the educators, and the determination to keep moving forward ensure that what has been started will be finished only when the entire district is working as a unit, kindergarten through graduation, to embed a twenty-first-century learning opportunity for each student personally.

Some might believe that this is already being done throughout districts nationally. However, as stated often, these attempts are on the right track, but there is not a cohesive and comprehensive effort to change the entire system, to eliminate the idea that the change is alternative, or to focus on a learning system that ensures independent student-centered education from the first day of kindergarten until the diploma is placed in the hand of the graduate.

This requires a reshaping of the paradigm. Pea Ridge, rather than being a model for an idea or experiment, has committed to be a leader for how an entire district can achieve this transformation for every learner and every teacher. The leadership of a forward-thinking superintendent, the commitment of principals and teachers, and the engagement of children and adolescents in the new paradigm create an opportunity for these students not previously known.

It can be done. And it can be done nationally. If we could project ourselves twenty-five years into the future, we would certainly see a much different school system across our nation. We will be changed. Since the latter part of the twentieth century, we've cried for the change, experimented with the change, and known the change is coming. But what we now see is that our "change" is in danger of quickly becoming an institutionalized "cycle." So it's time to change our paradigms about learning and teaching. No more programs, no more test runs, and no more waiting until every adult gets comfortable.

Transformation. Enough with the experiments.

NOTE

1. Portions of this chapter have been written with permission from leadership at Pea Ridge School District in Pea Ridge, Arkansas, and Responsive Education Solutions in Lewisville, Texas.

ABOUT THE AUTHOR

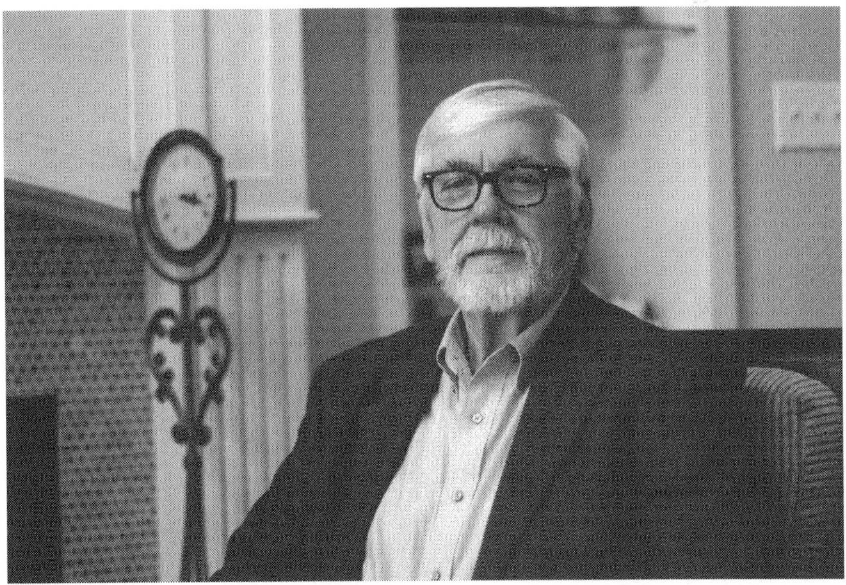

Merging years of work in the field with years of research can give an educator a unique perspective on the challenges currently facing education. Having worked with students and educators for almost forty years, Alan Wimberley has navigated tremendous change in learning environments and introduces this perspective consistently as an executive leader in education. In his area of expertise, current trends and issues, his work as a professor at the doctoral level has afforded him authentic opportunities to mentor administrators and teachers in K–12 and higher education.

Serving as a subject matter expert, professor, and dissertation chair for doctoral candidates, as well as being a course writer in twenty-first-century education for graduate students, Dr. Wimberley has connected his experience as a researcher and practitioner to teach, motivate, and encourage those who work with students every day. Countless numbers of educators, from elementary teachers to college professors, have been challenged and changed by the guiding principles in his work and his unwavering call to change how we think about teaching and learning.

Along with his writing, teaching, and speaking on current trends and issues, he also serves as an executive for one of the largest systems of nonprofit public charter schools in the nation. Each piece of his work calls for a transformation defined by the belief that only transformed educators can make it happen and transformed educators are sometimes hard to find.

Blending a natural sense of humor with a hunger to help teachers and students, Dr. Wimberley has been instrumental and influential in mentoring high-level educators to think more clearly and create campuses and classrooms where each student has greater opportunity. His most significant work is the relationships he forges between those inside and outside the education reform movement to create the best environments for learners.

In all this, he's constantly reminded that he is, first and foremost, a grandparent who should be doing whatever he can to make learning environments in the future better; for his grandchildren, for teachers, and for generations of learners that have yet to sit in our classrooms. Driven by his passion to help parents, advise policymakers, and teach educators, he balances what we do today on one important thought: *What will our classrooms be doing in thirty years and what does this generation of educators need to do today to make that happen?*

Dr. Alan Wimberley is a motivating speaker, passionate writer, and energetic creator of authentic learning systems. You can find his writings about reshaping the paradigms of teaching and learning at www.alanwimberley.com or visit the website of Responsive Education Solutions at www.ResponsiveEd.com, where he serves under the leadership of the CEO as the chief education architect for hundreds of educators. You can also see evidence of the principles in this book at www.valueaddeducation.com. For those interested in his availability for speaking engagements, shared and mutual efforts, or additional opportunities, he can be contacted at reshaping.ed@gmail.com.

Made in the USA
Columbia, SC
29 March 2019